Picture This!

Learning English Through Pictures

2

TIM HARRIS   **ALLAN ROWE**

PEARSON
Longman

Picture This! Learning English Through Pictures 2

Pearson Education, 10 Bank Street, White Plains, NY 10606

Cover illustration: Allan Rowe
Text design: Tim Harris
Text composition: Jacqueline Tobin
Text font: 13/15 Times Roman, 13/15 Helvetica
Text art: Allan Rowe
Editor: Suzi Wong

Library of Congress Cataloging-in-Publication Data

Harris, Tim (Timothy A.)
  Picture this! : learning English through pictures, 2 / Tim Harris,
Allan Rowe.
      p. cm.
  Level 2 of a multiskills course for beginners.
  ISBN 0-13-170339-0 (student book) -- ISBN 0-13-170341-2 (teacher's
edition) -- ISBN 0-13-170342-0 (audio cd's)
  1. English language--Textbooks for foreign speakers. 2. English
language--Grammar--Problems, exercises, etc. I. Rowe, Allan. II. Title.

  PE1128.H3493 2006
  428.2'4--dc22

                          2006020051

Printed in the United States of America
1 2 3 4 5 6 7 8 9 10-CRK-10 09 08 07 06

To our families

CONTENTS

PREFACE

Picture This! is a two-level multi-skills course for beginning students of English. This innovative course enables students to master the basics, so they can use English effectively for everyday situations.

APPROACH AND METHODOLOGY

The ability of our students to communicate in English involves two tasks at the same time: (1) deciding what they want to say and (2) using the appropriate language to express their thoughts. It's much easier for them to do both things at once if the second task can be done automatically. Our first priority, therefore, is to help students "automatize" basic structures and high-frequency vocabulary, the "core language" they need for communication.

Automatization is the ability of students to remember information and perform tasks without having to stop and think about what they are doing. When information or tasks are automatized, using this information and performing these tasks is almost as effortless as breathing. To help beginning students automatize the core language, *Picture This!* provides intensive practice based on principles of learning that promote memory.

Memory – central to all types of learning – is especially important in language learning because it determines how well students are able to use the language after they leave the classroom. If we understand how memory can be made stronger – for example, by visualization, by rehearsal, by transformation, or by writing – we can design lessons that will help our students improve their memory for the material they must learn. To enhance memory, *Picture This!* uses a range of picture-based lessons in an integrated skills approach to learning.

PICTURE-BASED LESSONS: It is all too easy for students to forget language or concepts that are "explained" in class. It is much easier to remember concepts that are shown or demonstrated, and pictures, by their very nature, show instead of tell. The lively and engaging illustrations in *Picture This!* make it easy for students to learn and remember the words for people, places, objects, and characteristics. The artwork also provides effective and meaningful practice with basic structures and language functions. Learning experts tell us an excellent way to remember something is to change it, to transform it in some way. To help students remember new grammar and vocabulary, *Picture This!* asks students to express in words the instructional information contained in the pictures. By taking something *visual* and making it *verbal*, the students are transforming information and filing it in their active working memory.

INTEGRATED SKILLS: In *Picture This!* the four skills of language learning (listening, speaking, reading, and writing) are usually combined in the same lesson. A typical lesson contains several pictures demonstrating a particular grammatical structure or language function. The students hear the target structure as they listen to conversations about the pictures, and they repeat the questions and answers they hear on the recordings. The students are encouraged to recreate the conversations with information provided by the pictures. They also write the sentences containing the target structure, which they then read aloud. By the end of the lesson, all four skills have been applied to learning a single structure, and when this happens, student retention increases dramatically.

Picture This! offers a true integrated skills approach to learning, with lessons designed in such a way that one skill improves another. Particular attention is given to integrating the writing skill, as writing can do so much to foster acquisition of the other skills. For example, it's a great advantage when students get in the habit of writing down their "talk" because this makes their thinking – and their mistakes – visible. So we suggest having students go to the board and write the language forms they have been practicing orally. With a little assistance, students are able to correct their own mistakes in grammar and spelling. This opportunity enables students to take risks, to monitor their progress, and to improve their ability to communicate – both orally and in writing.

LEARNING ENGLISH THROUGH PICTURES: The detailed illustrations in *Picture This!* make key vocabulary easily comprehensible to students, so they can perform a range of meaningful tasks from the first day of class. Packed with visual information, the illustrations provide frequent opportunities to go beyond the lesson on the page and engage in more spontaneous, less-structured activities. The illustrations present a cast of colorful characters in all kinds of situations, often humorous, for students to talk about. Having conversations about fictional characters paves the way for students to talk about their own life experiences. The warm, evocative illustrations in *Picture This!* make learning English more personal and enjoyable for the students.

FREE EXPRESSION AND FLUENCY

Picture This! 2 takes advantage of the students' greater command of English at the high-beginning/low-intermediate level to provide more opportunities for free expression. For example, students learn to improvise conversations about a range of topics presented in the Student Book. In these unscripted conversations, students *initiate* as well as respond to questions about a particular topic. The ability of students to ask their own questions and follow up with more questions is an essential conversation skill that builds fluency.

We recognize that students need time to think about the questions they are going to ask as they break away from guided or scripted conversations and begin to engage in free conversations. For this reason, *Picture This! 2* encourages students to compose a few questions they can use to keep the conversation going. Writing down questions along with a few key words or comments about a given topic assures students they have something to say. This builds their confidence and increases their contributions. As students develop the habit of asking questions, they will rely less on their notes and have more spontaneous conversations and discussions.

Perhaps the best way to prepare students for free conversations is to have them write short compositions about topics they would enjoy discussing with their friends. *Picture This! 2* teaches students how to generate ideas and express themselves clearly in writing. When students write short compositions about personal matters, they get valuable practice using the kind of language – including grammatical structures and vocabulary – they will need when they have conversations about similar topics.

We know that talking about a particular subject makes it easier for students to write about it. It is equally true that language learners are more confident when they have conversations about topics they have written about. The continuous interplay between speaking and writing is a key feature of *Picture This! 2* that promotes the rapid development of both skills. This method enables students to carry on unscripted conversations and write original compositions, the kind of free expression that students need to build fluency.

WHAT EACH CHAPTER CONTAINS

Cartoon Story   The grammar of each chapter is introduced in an entertaining cartoon story that demonstrates the use of natural speech and conversational expressions. The stories personalize the themes and functions covered in the curriculum.

Grammar   Picture-based lessons provide thorough, systematic, and meaningful practice with the grammatical structures introduced in each chapter.

Listening   The listening activities are integrated with oral activities and writing exercises to develop students' ability to understand, reproduce, and remember what they hear.

Speaking   Students develop their speaking ability through a variety of activities including guided conversations, role plays, and free response questions that allow students to talk about themselves. Imaginative illustrations suggest many opportunities for creative language practice.

Reading   Various types of texts enable students to steadily develop their reading skills as they learn new grammar and vocabulary. Stimulating topics create motivated readers and opportunities for discussion.

Writing   The writing exercises reinforce core language and help students develop their listening, speaking, and reading skills.

Pronunciation   Each chapter includes a section with exercises that focus on pronunciation points, such as vowel and consonant sounds, plurals, stress and intonation.

Life Skills   Everyday life situations provide contexts for learning basic competencies in the areas that are most important to students: food, clothing, transportation, work, housing, and health care.

COURSE COMPONENTS:

The text of *Picture This!* is recorded on three CDs. An interleaved Teacher's Edition provides practical teaching tips, expansion activities, and answer keys.

CONTENTS

Chapter 1

▶ **TOPICS**

Restaurants

Your Neighborhood

▶ **GRAMMAR**

Adverbs of Frequency

Quantifiers:
A lot of/much/many
Only a few/only a little

▶ **FUNCTIONS**

Talking about feelings

Finding locations

Giving directions

Talking about quantity

Describing where you live

▶ **COMPOSITION**

Writing about your
neighborhood

▶ **PRONUNCIATION**

Stress

CARTOON STORY

▶ 🎧 *Mrs. Peel is having lunch at the Magnolia Restaurant. Listen. Listen and practice.*

▶ QUESTIONS

1. Why does Mrs. Peel call the waiter?
2. What does Mrs. Peel want?
3. Is the manager busy? What is the manager doing?
4. Does Fido like bones? What about soup?
5. What is your opinion of the Magnolia Restaurant?

▶ GROUP WORK • *Discuss these questions.*

• What's your favorite restaurant? Where is it? Is it expensive?
• What kind of food do they serve? What's your favorite dish?
• Why do you like this restaurant? Is it the food, the service, or the prices?

*service = the help they give you

FEELINGS

1. Mrs. Peel is upset.

2. Grover is happy.

3. Mark is sad.

4. Daisy is scared.

5. Lisa is excited.

6. Jason is embarrassed.

7. Suzi is nervous.

8. Mr. Ratcliff is worried.

9. Ana is disappointed.

▶ **PAIR WORK** • *Ask and answer questions about the pictures.*

1. Mrs. Peel

   A: **Why is Mrs. Peel upset?**

   B: **She's upset because there's a fly in her soup.**

FEELINGS

▶ **CLASS WORK** • *Look at the pictures. How do these people feel? Use the adjectives on page 4. More than one adjective is possible.*

▶ **PAIR WORK** • *Take turns asking questions about feelings.*

1. How do you feel when you go to the dentist? **I feel scared.** OR **I'm nervous.**
2. How do you feel when you have a birthday party and your friends don't come?
3. How do you feel when you're at a movie and the people next to you are talking?
4. How do you feel when the teacher asks a question and you don't know the answer?
5. How do you feel when your favorite team wins a big game?
6. How do you feel when your favorite team loses a big game?
7. How do you feel when you take a test?
8. How do you feel when someone gives you a compliment?
9. How do you feel when someone in your family is very sick?

ADVERBS OF FREQUENCY

▶ 🎧 *Listen. Listen and practice.*

GRAMMAR • Adverbs of Frequency

Adverbs of Frequency			
I	always usually often sometimes hardly ever never	take the bus.	100% ↑ | 0%

▶ **WRITING** • *Add adverbs of frequency to the sentences so they are true for you.*

Example: I wear a hat. <u>I sometimes wear a hat.</u> OR <u>I never wear a hat.</u>

1. I get up early in the morning. _____

2. I take a shower in the morning. _____

3. I eat breakfast. _____

4. I walk to school. _____

5. I study at the library. _____

6. I read the newspaper. _____

7. I watch TV after dinner. _____

8. I listen to classical music. _____

9. I go dancing on the weekend. _____

▶ **PAIR WORK** • *Ask and answer questions using adverbs of frequency.*

A: **Do you ever eat out?**
B: **Yes, I often eat out. OR No, I hardly ever eat out. I usually eat at home.**

1. Do you usually get up early?

2. Do you always brush your teeth?

3. Do you often wear jeans?

4. Do you ever take the bus?

5. Do you always do your homework?

6. Do you usually study at the library?

7. Do you often read the newspaper?

8. Do you sometimes listen to rock music?

9. Do you ever go dancing?

THE RAT RACE

▶ 🎧 *A day in the life of Felix Ratcliff. Listen. Listen and practice.*

GRAMMAR • Adverbs of Frequency

Adverbs of Frequency with Be			
I'm He's We're	always usually often sometimes hardly ever never	in a hurry.	100% ↑ 0%

▶ **WRITING** • *Add adverbs of frequency to the sentences so they are true for you.*

Example: I'm late to work. <u>I'm often late to work.</u> OR <u>I'm never late to work.</u>

1. I'm happy. _____

2. I'm sad. _____

3. I'm in a hurry. _____

4. I'm late to my English class. _____

5. I'm busy in the afternoon. _____

6. I'm stressed out. _____

7. I'm tired when I come home. _____

8. I'm at home in the evening. _____

9. I'm in bed by 11:00 pm. _____

▶ **PAIR WORK** • *Ask and answer questions using adverbs of frequency.*

A: **Are you often in a hurry?**
B: **Yes, I'm usually in a hurry.** OR **No, I'm hardly ever in a hurry.**

1. Are you usually happy?

2. Are you ever sad?

3. Are you often in a hurry?

4. Are you sometimes late to class?

5. Are you usually busy?

6. Are you ever stressed out?

7. Are you often tired when you come home?

8. Are you always at home in the evening?

9. Are you usually in bed by midnight?

▶ 🎧 *Listen and repeat the names of the places you see on the map.*

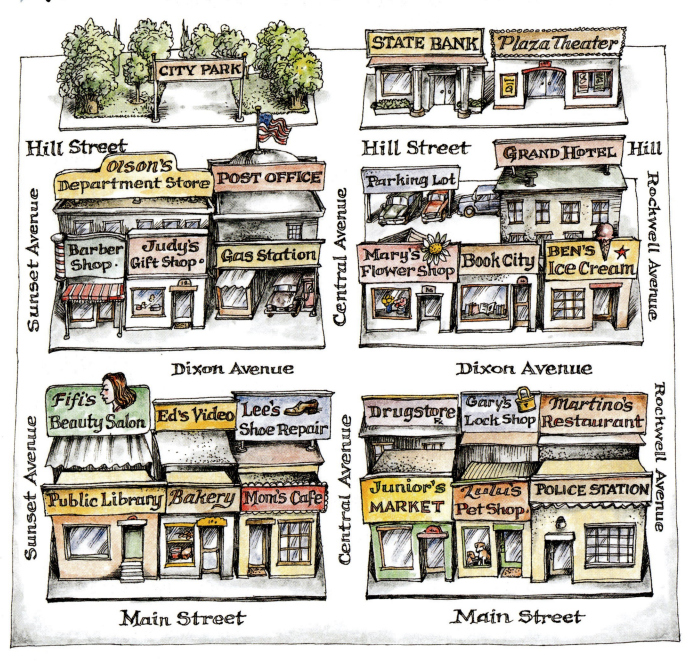

▶ **PAIR WORK** • *Ask and answer questions. Use **between, next to, across from,** and **on the corner of** in your answers.*

the police station

A: **Where's the police station?**

B: **It's on Main Street, *on the corner of* Main and Rockwell.**

Gary's Lock Shop

A: **Where is Gary's Lock Shop?**

B: **It's on Dixon Avenue, *between* the drugstore and Martino's Restaurant.**

1. the parking lot
2. Lulu's Pet Shop
3. Olson's Department Store
4. Lee's Shoe Repair
5. State Bank
6. Judy's Gift Shop
7. the post office
8. the bakery
9. Plaza Theater

LIFE SKILL • Giving Directions

walk up	turn right	on the right	next to	across from
walk down	turn left	on the left	between	on the corner of

Lulu's Pet Shop → Plaza Theater

▶ **CONVERSATION 1**

🎧 *Listen. Listen and practice.*

A: Excuse me. How do I get to the Plaza Theater from here?

B: Go to Rockwell Avenue and **turn left. Walk up** two blocks to Hill Street. The Plaza Theater is **on the corner of** Hill and Rockwell, **across from** the Grand Hotel.

A: Thank you.

▶ **CONVERSATION 2**

🎧 *Listen. Listen and practice.*

A: Excuse me. How do I get to Judy's Gift Shop from here?

B: **Walk down** Central Avenue one block to Dixon Avenue. **Turn right** and **walk down** Dixon Avenue. Judy's Gift Shop is **on the right, between** the gas station and the barbershop.

A: Thanks very much.

State Bank → Judy's Gift Shop

▶ 🎧 **DICTATION** • *Listen and write the directions from City Park to Lulu's Pet Shop.*

_____

_____

_____

▶ **PAIR WORK** • *Ask for and give directions. Use the conversations as models.*

1. Mom's Cafe → parking lot
2. Book City → Olson's Department Store
3. public library → Gary's Lock Shop
4. State Bank → bakery

5. Grand Hotel → Lee's Shoe Repair
6. Lulu's Pet Shop → City Park
7. barbershop → Fifi's Beauty Salon
8. post office → Book City

GRAMMAR • Quantifiers

COUNTABLES Affirmative		
There are	**a lot of** **many**	flowers. trees.

COUNTABLES Negative		
There aren't	**a lot of** **many**	flowers. trees.

UNCOUNTABLES Affirmative		
There's	**a lot of**	traffic. noise.

UNCOUNTABLES Negative		
There isn't	**much** **a lot of**	traffic. noise.

▶ 🎧 *Listen to what these people say about their neighborhoods. Listen and repeat.*

❑ My neighborhood is **beautiful**. The streets are clean, and there are **a lot of** flowers and trees.

❑ My neighborhood is **ugly**. The streets are dirty, and there aren't **many** flowers or trees.

❑ My neighbors are very **friendly**. I know **a lot of** people on my street.

❑ My neighbors aren't very friendly. I don't know **many** people on my street.

☐ It's very **convenient** where I live. There are **a lot of** stores nearby.

☐ It isn't very **convenient** where I live. There aren't **many** stores around here.

☐ I live on a **busy** street. There's **a lot of** traffic and noise.

☐ I live on a **quiet** street. There isn't **much** traffic or noise.

☐ This is an **interesting** place to live. There's **a lot** to do around here.

☐ This is a **boring** place to live. There isn't **much** to do around here.

▶ **DESCRIBE WHERE YOU LIVE** • *Put a check (✓) next to the statements that are true about your street or neighborhood. Then read the statements out loud.*

GRAMMAR • Quantifiers

▶ **PRACTICE** • *Describe the pictures using **a lot of**, **much** and **many**.*

1. people / bus stop

There are **a lot of** people at the bus stop.

2. gas / car

There isn't **much** gas in the car.

3. trees / mountain

There aren't **many** trees on the mountain.

4. water / river

5. food / table

6. people / meeting

7. traffic / Main Street

8. books / bookcase

9. soup / bowl

10. flowers / vase

11. apples / basket

12. orange juice / bottle

GRAMMAR • Quantifiers

| There are | **only (just) a few** | customers in Al's Cafe. |
| There's | **only (just) a little** | money in the cash register. |

▶ **WRITING** • *Complete the sentences about the objects in the picture using* ***a lot of***, ***only a few*** *and* ***only a little***. *Then read the sentences out loud.*

1. <u>There are only a few</u> customers in Al's Cafe.
2. <u>There's only a little</u> money in the cash register.
3. _____ trash in the trash can.
4. _____ soup in the pot.
5. _____ cookies in the jar.
6. _____ French fries on Joe's plate.
7. _____ ketchup in the bottle.
8. _____ ice cream in Sara's dish.
9. _____ flowers in the vase.
10. _____ coffee in the pot.
11. _____ dishes on the shelf.
12. _____ glasses on the shelf.

▶ **PAIR WORK** • *Ask and answer questions about the objects in the picture.*

soup / pot
A: **How much soup is in the pot?**
B: **Just a little.**

dishes / shelf
A: **How many dishes are on the shelf?**
B: **A lot.**

glasses / shelf
A: **How many glasses are on the shelf?**
B: **Just a few.**

1. customers / Al's Cafe
2. money / cash register
3. trash / trash can
4. cookies / jar
5. French fries / Joe's plate
6. ketchup / bottle
7. ice cream / Sara's dish
8. flowers / vase
9. coffee / pot

WHERE YOU LIVE

▶ 🎧 *Listen and read.*

Nancy and Jack are friends. Nancy lives with her family in a small town. Jack lives with his parents in a big city. Today Nancy is sitting on her front porch writing a letter to Jack. She's describing her house and the street where she lives.

▶ **WARM UP QUESTIONS**

1. Where is Nancy?
2. What is she doing?
3. What are her neighbors like?
4. What does Nancy's house look like?

▶ 🎧 **DICTATION** • *Listen to Nancy's description of the place where she lives. Listen again and write each sentence, line by line.*

_____

_____

_____

_____

_____

_____

YOUR NEIGHBORHOOD

▶ 🎧 *Jack is calling Nancy long distance. Listen. Listen and practice.*

Hello?

NANCY: Hello?

JACK: Nancy, it's Jack.

NANCY: Hi, Jack. How are you doing?

JACK: Fine. I got your letter yesterday. It sounds like you live in a nice neighborhood.

NANCY: Yes, it's very nice.

Nancy, it's Jack.

▶ 🎧 *Look at this picture as you listen to the rest of the conversation.*

▶ **QUESTIONS**

1. What's it like where Jack lives? Is it crowded? noisy? fun?
2. Does Jack have friendly neighbors? What's the manager like?
3. Is there much to do where Jack lives?
4. What is Jack's favorite place to hang out? Why does he like it there?

▶ **COMPOSITION 1** • *On a separate piece of paper, write a 50-75 word description of Jack's neighborhood. Look at the picture and the questions for ideas. Begin like this:* Jack lives in an old apartment building downtown.

▶ **PAIR WORK** • *Talk about your neighborhood. What's it like? Do you know your neighbors? What are they like? Is there much to do in your neighborhood? Where do you hang out? Do you like your neighborhood? Why or why not?*

▶ **COMPOSITION 2** • *Write a 50-75 word description of your neighborhood.*

VOCABULARY

NOUNS

Feelings
disappointed
embarrassed
excited
happy
nervous
sad
scared
upset
worried

Other
bone
cash register
customer
fly
interview
manager
river
service
trash

QUANTIFIERS
a few
a little
a lot of
many
much

ADJECTIVES
convenient
delicious

VERBS
feel
prefer
relax

PRONOUNS
anything
nobody

DETERMINER
another

EXPRESSIONS

Talking about quantity
How much...?   Just a little.
How many...?   Just a few.

Directions
Walk up.   Turn right.   It's on the right.
Walk down.   Turn left.   It's on the left.

You're late!
  I'm sorry.

Felix doesn't look good.
  He's stressed out.

Look, Dad!
  Don't bother me. I'm busy.

Are you okay?
  I'm worried about these bills.

What's wrong with him?
  He's in a bad mood.

What's the problem?
  Nobody calls me.

What about you?
  I'm going on a date.

You look great.
  Thanks.

Why don't you try it?
  That sounds like a good idea.

It's a good way to relax.
  You're right.

Don't just stand there. Do something!
  I'm in a hurry.

It's on Hill Street.
  Are you sure?

STRESS

▶ **A** 🎧 *Listen to the stressed vowels. Listen and repeat.*

wíndow	ex**pén**sive	re**láx**
sérvice	im**pór**tant	for**gét**
mánager	edu**cá**tion	gui**tár**
cústomer	cafe**tér**ia	ma**chín**e

▶ **B** 🎧 *Listen and mark the stressed vowels. Then read these words out loud.*

computer	favorite	comfortable
exercise	hotel	cartoon
understand	personality	entertainment
department	introduce	wonderful

▶ **C** 🎧 *Listen. Notice the main stress in these sentences. Listen and practice.*

NANCY: He**lló**?

JACK: **Nán**cy, it's **Jáck**.

NANCY: **Hí, Jáck**. **Hów** are you **dó**ing?

JACK: **Fíne**. I **gót** your **lét**ter **yés**terday. It **sóunds** like you **líve** in a **níce néigh**borhood.

NANCY: **Yés**, it's **vér**y nice.

▶ **D** 🎧 *Listen and mark the stress in these sentences. Then practice the conversation with a partner.*

MRS. PEEL: Waiter! There's a fly in my soup!

WAITER: Are you sure?

MRS. PEEL: Take a look.

WAITER: I don't see anything.

MRS. PEEL: Take another look.

WAITER: Oh, I see it now. You're right. There is a fly in your soup.

MRS. PEEL: Well, don't just stand there. Do something!

GRAMMAR SUMMARY

Adverbs of Frequency with Action Verbs

	always usually often sometimes hardly ever never	get up early. read the newspaper. take the bus.
I		

Adverbs of Frequency with *Be*

I'm	always usually often sometimes hardly ever never	busy.
He's		in a hurry.
We're		late.

QUANTIFIERS: A lot / much / many

COUNTABLES Affirmative

I have	a lot of many	books. friends.

COUNTABLES Negative

I don't have	a lot of many	books. friends.

UNCOUNTABLES Affirmative

There's	a lot of	traffic. noise.

UNCOUNTABLES Negative

We don't have	much a lot of	food. money.

QUANTIFIERS: Only a few / only a little

COUNTABLES

There are	only a few	cups glasses	on the shelf.

UNCOUNTABLES

There's	only a little	milk cheese	on the table.

CONTENTS

Chapter 2

CARTOON STORY

🎧 *Lulu is going on a blind date with Mike Franken. Listen. Listen and practice.*

▶ **THINK ABOUT IT** • *Mike says and does a lot of things to impress Lulu on their first date. What's your opinion of Mike's words and actions? Read each sentence out loud and say: "That's good." OR "That's a mistake." OR "That's not important."*

1. Mike arrives on time for his date with Lulu.
2. Mike tells Lulu that she looks beautiful.
3. Mike brings Lulu a bouquet of flowers.
4. Mike opens the car door for Lulu.
5. Mike takes Lulu to an expensive restaurant.
6. Mike tells Lulu that he works for a large corporation and he's doing "very well."
7. Mike takes a phone call from his boss while he's having dinner with Lulu.
8. Mike tells Lulu that he loves cats and he reads Shakespeare.
9. Mike shows Lulu that he's a good dancer.
10. Mike kisses Lulu's hand at the end of their date.

▶ **GROUP DISCUSSION** • *How do men and women try to impress each other? Are they always honest? Do you think Mike Franken is honest with Lulu? What's your opinion of Mike? What's your opinion of Lulu? Do you have advice for Lulu?*

GRAMMAR • Like To

LIKE TO Affirmative		
He She	likes to	get up early. exercise. do housework.
I You We They	like to	

Negative		
He She	doesn't like to	get up early. exercise. do housework.
I You We They	don't like to	

▶ **WRITING** • *Write a sentence about each picture. Use the affirmative or negative form of **like to** with one of these verbs or expressions:* **do housework, dress up, eat alone, exercise, get up early, go hiking, shop, stand in line**. *After you finish, read the sentences out loud.*

1. He likes to get up early.

2. They don't like to stand in line.

3. _____

4. _____

5. _____

6. _____

7. _____

I'll take it.   ·Department Store·

8. _____

▶ **WRITING** • *Write true sentences about yourself. Begin each sentence with* **I like to** *or* **I don't like to**. *After you finish, read the sentences out loud.*

Example: shop   I like to shop.   OR   I don't like to shop. _____

1. get up early _____

2. do housework _____

3. exercise _____

4. dress up _____

5. dance _____

▶ **PAIR WORK** • *Ask your partner five questions starting with* **Do you like to...?**

Example: shop
Student A: **Do you like to shop?**
Student B: **Yes, I do.** OR **No, I don't.**

WHAT DO YOU LIKE TO DO?

▶ CONVERSATION 1

🎧 *Listen. Listen and practice.*

SUZI: What do you like to do on the weekend, Amy?

AMY: I like to play soccer.

SUZI: Oh, really? What position do you play?

AMY: I'm the goalie.

SUZI: Where do you play?

AMY: At Plummer Park. It's a great place for soccer.

SUZI: That sounds like fun.

AMY: Yeah, we have a good time.

▶ CONVERSATION 2

🎧 *Listen. Listen and practice.*

CARLOS: What do you like to do in your free time, Henry?

HENRY: I like to hear live music.

CARLOS: Oh, really? Where do you go to hear live music?

HENRY: I go to concerts and music festivals.

CARLOS: What kind of music do you like?

HENRY: All kinds – rock, country, jazz – but my favorite is blues.

CARLOS: Me, too. Do you like Jesse Winfield?

HENRY: Of course! He's the best!

▶ **THINK ABOUT IT** • *In the conversations above, Suzi and Carlos ask questions to get more information about their friends' interests. What questions does Suzi ask Amy in the first conversation? What questions does Carlos ask Henry?*

▶ **WHAT ARE YOUR INTERESTS?** • *Check (✓) the things you like to do.*

❑ read
❑ shop
❑ cook

❑ listen to music
❑ go dancing
❑ play the piano

❑ go to museums
❑ play a sport
❑ go hiking

❑ take photographs
❑ work in the garden
❑ spend time with friends

▶ **PAIR WORK** • *Talk with your partner about your interests. To get more information, ask each other questions beginning with **What, Where, Who, What kind of, How often.***

GRAMMAR

PRESENT CONTINUOUS	SIMPLE PRESENT
He's taking a nap.	He takes a nap every afternoon.
They're painting their house.	They paint their house once a year.

▶ 🎧 *Listen. Listen and repeat.*   ▶ **PAIR WORK** • *Practice the conversations.*

▶ **WRITING** • *Complete the answers using these verbs:* **brush, call, make, paint, play, read, take, wash, watch**.

What's your husband doing?

He's taking a nap. He takes a nap every afternoon.

What are the neighbors doing?

They're painting their house. They paint their house once a year.

What's Luisa doing?

 She's making the bed.

 She makes the bed every day.

What are Bob and Alice doing?

_____ their car.

_____ their car twice a week.

What's Grover doing?

_____ the newspaper.

_____ the newspaper every morning.

⑤

What's Suzi doing?

_____ her teeth.

_____ her teeth twice a day.

⑥

What are Jack and Jill doing?

_____ tennis.

_____ tennis three times a week.

⑦

What's Jason doing?

_____ his girlfriend.

_____ his girlfriend all the time.

⑧

What are Pete and Fred doing?

_____ football on TV.

_____ football every Sunday.

⑨

▶ **CLASS ACTIVITY** • *Talk about Mr. Little's daily routine. What does he do every day?*

▶ **QUESTIONS**

1. Why doesn't Mr. Little like his daily routine? Give some examples.
2. Why does the boss yell, "Get back to work!"?
3. Does Mr. Little daydream that he's a rock star or a super hero?
4. What do you daydream about?

▶ 🎧 **DICTATION** • *Listen to the story about Mr. Little. Listen again and write what you hear on a separate piece of paper.*

CLASS DISCUSSION • *Why does Mr. Little enjoy his "perfect day" so much? What happens on his perfect day that's better than an ordinary day in his life?*

COMPOSITION 1 • *Write a short story about Mr. Little's "perfect day." Use the pictures for ideas.*

GROUP WORK • *Discuss your "perfect day." What happens?*

COMPOSITION 2 • *Write a short story about your "perfect day."*

CARTOON STORY • Taking the Bus

▶ 🎧 *Mary Chen hardly ever takes the bus, so this morning she asks a man at the bus stop for information. His name is Fred Barnes. Listen. Listen and practice.*

A Car Is Too Much Trouble

▶ 🎧 *Listen to Fred say why he doesn't like to drive a car. Listen and practice.*

Traffic is getting worse and worse.
Car repairs cost a lot of money.
Gasoline is very expensive.
It's hard to find a place to park.
There are too many crazy drivers.
I'm afraid of getting in an accident.

▶ **WRITING** • *Using Fred's comments, write an appropriate sentence for each picture.*

1. <u>Gasoline is very expensive.</u>　　　2. _____

3. _____　　　4. _____

5. _____　　　6. _____

MAIN IDEA vs. DETAILS

A What's happening in the picture?

B Which sentence gives the best description of the picture?

1. Maria and Carlos are sitting under a maple tree.
2. Maria and Carlos are enjoying a picnic in the park.
3. It's a beautiful, sunny day.

Sentence #2 is the best because it tells the **main idea** of the picture – two people enjoying a picnic in the park. Sentences #1 and #3 describe **details** in the picture that tell more about the **main idea**.

C Paragraphs are like pictures; they also have **main ideas** and **details**. Read the paragraph below about Amos Boone and underline the **main idea**.

   Amos Boone has a tough job. He's a bus driver in a big city, and he often drives in heavy traffic. It's hard for Amos to stay on schedule, especially during the rush hour. Amos has to be careful because there are a lot of bad drivers, and he doesn't want to have an accident. In addition, the passengers give Amos a lot of trouble. They eat on the bus. They play loud music. They even try to talk to Amos while he's driving. No wonder Amos feels stressed out at the end of the day.

What's the **main idea** of the paragraph?

D Write two detail sentences that tell more about the main idea.

Detail: _____

Detail: _____

TOPIC SENTENCES

A A **topic sentence** states the main idea of a paragraph. In the paragraph below, the topic sentence is missing. Read the paragraph.

_____.

He never smiles. He never talks to his neighbors. He just sits on the porch with his cats. Mr. Ruffcorn doesn't have any friends. His only companions are his cats. Mr. Ruffcorn likes cats more than he likes people.

Which of the sentences below makes the best **topic sentence**?

1. Many people live alone.
2. Mr. Ruffcorn frowns a lot.
3. Mr. Ruffcorn isn't very friendly.

B Let's see why one sentence makes a better topic sentence than the others.

- Sentence #1 doesn't work because the paragraph isn't about people in general; it's about one man – Mr. Ruffcorn.

- Sentence #2 states that Mr. Ruffcorn frowns a lot. That's an interesting detail, but it isn't the main idea of the paragraph.

- Sentence #3 is the best because it's the only one that states the main idea: _Mr. Ruffcorn isn't very friendly._ This is more than a detail. It's the subject of the paragraph.

Write topic sentence #3 at the beginning of the paragraph about Mr. Ruffcorn.

C The topic sentence is also missing in the paragraph about Jason and Lisa below. Working with a partner, think of a good topic sentence and write it down.

_____.

He calls her every day. He gives her flowers and chocolates. He even keeps a picture of Lisa in his wallet. He looks at her picture all the time. Jason thinks Lisa is the most wonderful girl in the world.

SUPPORTING DETAILS

There's food everywhere.

It's dark inside.

It has large windows.

The sink is full of dirty dishes.

There's lots of sunlight.

There's one small window in the corner.

A mountain of trash sits in the corner.

A vase with pretty flowers sits on the table.

The only piece of furniture is a little bed.

▶ **WRITING** • *The details in a paragraph support (tell more about) the main idea. Add three supporting details from the box to each topic sentence below.*

1. Our neighbor's living room is very cheerful.

   It has large windows.

   _____

   _____

   _____

2. My uncle has a messy kitchen.

   _____

   _____

   _____

   _____

3. Ms. Flint's bedroom is depressing.

   _____

   _____

   _____

   _____

YOUR FAVORITE ROOM

▶ **CLASS ACTIVITY** • *Tell the location of the things you see in Mary's living room.*

Examples: There's a table next to the sofa. There are some photos on the wall.

▶ **WARM UP QUESTIONS**

1. Where is Mary sitting?
2. What is she doing?
3. Is she having a good time? How do you know?

▶ 🎧 **DICTATION** • *Listen to Mary. Listen again and write down what she says.*

_____

_____

_____

_____

_____

_____

_____

▶ **COMPOSITION** • *Write a paragraph about the room you like most in your house or apartment. Think about these questions before you start writing.*

• What kind of furniture do you have in this room?
• Is there a telephone, a computer, a TV set or a stereo in this room?
• What do you like to do in this room?
• Why is this room your favorite?

VOCABULARY

NOUNS

advice
author
collection
companion
corporation
fare
festival
maple tree
mistake
museum
sink
sunlight
super hero

VERBS

brag
daydream

ADJECTIVES

careful
crazy
dark
fabulous
full
playful
special
tough

ADVERBS

especially
normally
whenever

DETERMINER

which

PREPOSITION

inside

EXPRESSIONS

I'm doing very well.
   Good for you.

Let's dance.
   I'd love to.

A blind date.
   That sounds like fun.

You're right on time.
   So are you.

How much is the fare?
   A dollar twenty.

They give him trouble.
   He has to be careful.

He's the best!
   I'm impressed!

Traffic is getting worse.
   Oh, really?

In addition…
   What else?

Let's talk.
   Get back to work!

to dress up
to make the bed
to take a nap
to spend time
to stand in line

to get off the bus
to get in an accident

The rush hour.
Right on schedule.

PRONUNCIATION

▶ **A** 🎧 *Listen and repeat.*

/ε/

1. bed	4. yes	7. best
2. men	5. get	8. leather
3. pet	6. help	9. sweater

▶ **B** 🎧 *Listen and repeat.*

/ey/

1. make	4. name	7. mail
2. late	5. place	8. wait
3. face	6. grape	9. paint

▶ **C** 🎧 *Listen to each pair of words. Listen again and repeat.*

1. a. men   b. main

2. a. pen   b. pain

3. a. net   b. Nate

4. a. pepper   b. paper

5. a. sell   b. sale

6. a. test   b. taste

▶ **D** 🎧 *Look at the words in Part C. Listen and* (circle) *the words you hear.*

▶ **E** 🎧 *Listen and practice.*

1. Ben has a date with Jenny Lane.
2. The men are waiting for the next train.
3. Let's take our vacation in September.
4. Fred hates rainy weather.
5. Fresh tomatoes taste the best.
6. Betty makes great lemonade.

GRAMMAR SUMMARY

LIKE TO Affirmative		
He She	likes to	get up early. exercise. do housework.
I You We They	like to	

Negative			
He She	doesn't (does not)	like to	get up early. exercise. do housework.
I You We They	don't (do not)		

Interrogative			
Does	he she	like to	get up early? exercise? do housework?
Do	I you we they		

Short Answers							
Yes,	he she	does.		No,	he she	doesn't.
	I you we they	do.			I you we they	don't.

PRESENT CONTINUOUS
She's making the bed.
They're washing their car.

SIMPLE PRESENT
She makes the bed every day.
They wash their car twice a week.

CONTENTS

Chapter 3

CARTOON STORY

▶ 🎧 *Sara, Joe, and Eddie are making plans for the weekend. Listen. Listen and practice.*

▶ QUESTIONS

1. What do Sara and her friends want to do this weekend?
2. Is Sara's house a good place for a party? Why or why not?
3. What is a potluck party?
4. Why does Joe have to go now?

GRAMMAR • *Can*

CAN Affirmative		
He She I You We They	can	swim.

Negative		
He She I You We They	can't (cannot)	swim.

▶ **WRITING** • *Write a sentence below each picture using* **can** *or* **can't** *with one of these verbs:* **play, swim, cook, reach, sleep, repair, dance, move, ride, sing.** *After you finish, read the sentences out loud.*

1. <u>He can cook.</u>

2. <u>They can't move the piano.</u>

3. _____

4. _____

5. _____

6. _____

7. _____

8. _____

9. _____

10. _____

▶ **WRITING** • *Write true sentences about yourself. Begin each sentence with* **I can** *or* **I can't**. *After you finish, read the sentences out loud.*

Example: run fast <u>I can run fast.</u>_____

   OR <u>I can't run fast.</u>_____

1. ride a horse_____

2. speak French _____

3. sing_____

4. do the tango _____

5. play tennis _____

6. swim_____

7. cook _____

8. drive a truck_____

"She can run fast."

▶ **PAIR WORK** • *Ask your partner five questions starting with* **Can you...?**

Example: run fast
Student A: **Can you run fast?**
Student B: **Yes, I can.** OR **No, I can't.**

GRAMMAR • *Have to*

HAVE TO Affirmative		
He She	has to	get up early.
I You We They	have to	make breakfast. go to work.

Negative				
He She	doesn't (does not)			get up early.
I You We They	don't (do not)	have to		make breakfast. go to work.

▶ **WRITING** • *Look at the pictures and answer the questions using* **has to** *or* **have to**. *After you finish, pair up and read the sentences out loud.*

1. Why can't Ben and Sadie watch TV now?

   <u>They have to feed the chickens.</u>

2. Why can't Richard play golf today?

   _____

3. Why can't Ms. Davis talk on the phone now?

   _____

4. Why can't Sonia and Miguel go to the movies?

   _____

5. Why can't Mr. Brandon go home now?

_____

6. Why can't Mr. and Mrs. Wong see their friends today?

_____

7. Why can't Mrs. Wingate leave now?

_____

8. Why can't Sam read the newspaper now?

_____

▶ **WRITING** • _Write true sentences about yourself. Begin each sentence with_ **I have to** _or_ **I don't have to**. _After you finish, read the sentences out loud._

Example: get up early _I have to get up early._ _____

            OR _I don't have to get up early._ _____

1. make breakfast _____

2. wash the dishes _____

3. go to school every day _____

4. study tonight _____

5. take a test next week _____

▶ **PAIR WORK** • _Ask your partner five questions starting with_ **Do you have to...?**

Example: get up early
Student A: **Do you have to get up early?**
Student B: **Yes, I do.** OR **No, I don't.**

GRAMMAR • *Want to*

WANT TO Affirmative		
He She	wants to	go home. watch TV. eat popcorn.
I You We They	want to	

Negative			
He She	doesn't (does not)	want to	go home. watch TV. eat popcorn.
I You We They	don't (do not)		

▶ **WRITING** • *Write a sentence below each picture using the affirmative or negative form of* **want to**. *After you finish, read the sentences out loud.*

1. <u>She wants to take a vacation.</u>

2. <u>They don't want to join the army.</u>

Get up!

3. _____

4. _____

5. _____

6. _____

7. _____

8. _____

▶ **WRITING** • *Write true sentences about yourself. Begin each sentence with* **I want to** *or* **I don't want to**. *After you finish, read the sentences out loud.*

Example: be a movie star   I want to be a movie star.

OR   I don't want to be a movie star.

1. go to Hollywood _____

2. make millions _____

3. live in a big house _____

4. wear fancy clothes _____

5. eat peaches and cream _____

▶ **PAIR WORK** • *Ask your partner five questions starting with* **Do you want to...?**

Example: be a movie star
Student A: **Do you want to be a movie star?**
Student B: **Yes, I do.** OR **No, I don't. I want to be a truck driver.**

▶ **WHAT'S GOING ON?** • *Look at the picture. What's happening?*

▶ **WARM UP**

1. What movie is playing at the Plaza Theater?
2. Who's in it?
3. What does Karen want to do?
4. What does she have to do first?

▶ 🎧 **DICTATION** • *Listen. Listen and write.*

_____

_____

_____

_____

_____

_____

_____

_____

▶ WHAT'S GOING ON? • *Look at the picture. What's happening?*

▶ WARM UP

1. Where is Billy?
2. Why is he looking out the window?
3. What does Billy want to do?
4. Why is Billy's mother upset?
5. What does she want Billy to do?

▶ COMPOSITION • *Write a 40-60 word story about the picture.*

_____

_____

_____

_____

_____

_____

_____

_____

Health Problems

▶ 🎧 *Look and listen.*

▶ **WRITING** • *Complete the sentences with **her, him, them** and **He, She, They**. After you finish, pair up and read the sentences out loud.*

1. What's wrong with __them__?
   __They__ have sore feet.

2. What's the matter with _____?
   _____ has a headache.

3. What's wrong with _____?
   _____ has a sore throat.

4. What's wrong with _____?
   _____ have sore knees.

5. What's the matter with _____?
   _____ has a backache.

6. What's the matter with _____?
   _____ has a stomachache.

▶ 🎧 PARTS OF THE BODY
Listen and repeat.

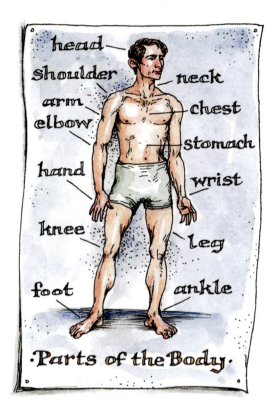

head
shoulder
neck
arm
elbow
chest
stomach
hand
wrist
knee
leg
foot
ankle

· Parts of the Body ·

▶ 🎧 CONVERSATION • *Listen and practice.*

What's wrong with him?

His arm hurts.

CLINIC

① ② ③ ④

▶ PAIR WORK 1 • *Talk about the other patients who are waiting in the doctor's office.*

A: What's wrong with him/her?

B: His/Her _____ hurts.

▶ 🎧 MAKING AN APPOINTMENT
Listen. Listen and practice.

85

Doctor's Office

Receptionist

A: Hello. This is Eddie Mobley. I'm a patient of Dr. Feelgood.

B: Yes, Mr. Mobley. What's the matter?

A: My knee hurts. I need an appointment with Dr. Feelgood.

B: Can you come in this afternoon at 2 o'clock?

A: No, I can't. I'm busy this afternoon.

B: Let's see… how about tomorrow morning at ten?

A: Tomorrow at ten? Yes. That's fine. Thank you.

B: You're welcome. See you then. Good-bye.

A: Good-bye.

▶ PAIR WORK 2 • *Have a similar conversation. Make an appointment to see Dr. Feelgood. Use your own information.*

▶ **CLASS ACTIVITY** • *What are these people doing that is good or bad for their health?*

1. He's eating vegetables. That's good.   2. She's drinking a lot of soda. That's bad.

eating vegetables

drinking a lot of soda

exercising •

working too much

• sleeping •

• smoking •

• laughing •

eating junk food

drinking water •

▶ **WRITING** • *List three things that are good for your health and three things that are bad for your health.*

GOOD	**BAD**
Example: <u>eating vegetables</u>	Example: <u>drinking a lot of soda</u>
1. _____	1. _____
2. _____	2. _____
3. _____	3. _____

▶ 🎧 *Listen. Listen and practice.*

Adverbs of Frequency	
100% ↑	always
	usually
	often
	sometimes
	hardly ever
0%	never

Which coffee is the best? There are so many kinds. This is really difficult...

You worry too much about little things. It's just coffee.

▶ **WRITING** • *Write true sentences about yourself using adverbs of frequency. After you finish, read the sentences out loud.*

Example: drink coffee   <u>I often drink coffee.</u> OR <u>I never drink coffee.</u>

1. eat junk food   _____

2. sleep eight hours at night   _____

3. exercise in the morning   _____

4. work too much   _____

5. worry about little things   _____

6. laugh out loud   _____

7. drink soda   _____

8. eat fruit and vegetables   _____

▶ **CLASS ACTIVITY** • *Answer these questions about your lifestyle.*

1.   What are your favorite foods?
2.   What fruits and vegetables do you like?
3.   Do you sometimes eat junk food? What kind?
4.   How often do you exercise? Every day? Three times a week? Never?
5.   What kind of exercise do you get?
6.   Do you play any sports? Which ones? How often?
7.   What time do you usually go to bed at night?
8.   How many hours do you sleep?
9.   How often do you see your friends? Every day? Now and then? Hardly ever?
10.   What activities do you like to do with your friends?

▶ **PAIR WORK** • *Ask your partner the questions above and take notes. Then tell the class three things you know about your partner's lifestyle.*

▶ 🎧 **DICTATION** • *Listen. Listen and write.*

_____

_____

_____

_____

_____

_____

_____

▶ **CLASS ACTIVITY** • *Look at the picture of Maynard. How is he different from Mike?*

▶ **COMPOSITION** • *Write a paragraph about Maynard on a separate sheet of paper.*
Use this topic sentence: <u>Maynard doesn't take care of his health.</u>

PRE-WRITING: Clustering

▶ **A** Before writing a composition, you must have something to say. You must have ideas. The best way to get ideas is by *clustering*. First, write the main idea, a word or phrase, on a sheet of paper and circle it. Then write down everything that comes to your mind, everything you can think of. To see how it works, look at Sonia's cluster. The main idea is **my lifestyle**.

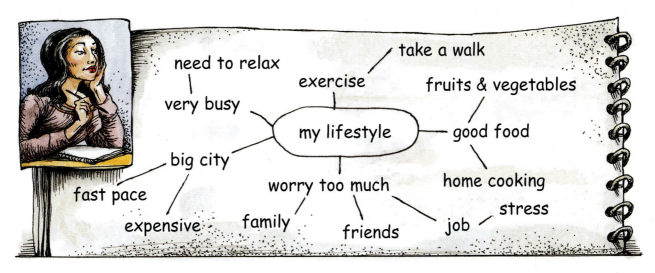

▶ **B** Read Sonia's short composition about her lifestyle and her health. Notice how she uses some of the ideas from the cluster in her composition.

I try to take good care of my health. I exercise every day and
eat foods that are good for me. My problem is that I worry
too much. I worry about my family, my friends and my job.
I even worry about little things like which coffee I should buy.
I worry so much that I can't sleep at night. I know that
all this worrying is bad for my health. I hope some day I
can learn to relax and enjoy life.

▶ **C** In a few minutes, you're going to write a short composition about your lifestyle. But first, start clustering ideas. Write **my lifestyle** on a separate sheet of paper. Then write down everything about your lifestyle that is good or bad for your health. What do the details in your cluster say about your lifestyle? Is it healthy or unhealthy? Do you take good care of your health or not? Choose one of the topic sentences below and write a short composition about your lifestyle and your health.

Topic Sentences

• I try to take good care of my health.
• I don't take very good care of my health.

VOCABULARY

NOUNS

Parts of the body

ankle
arm
chest
elbow
foot
hand
head
knee
leg
neck
shoulder
stomach
wrist

Other

appointment
backache
cream
energy
health
house
lifestyle
patient
potluck
tango

ADJECTIVES

healthy ≠ unhealthy

EXPRESSIONS

Talking about physical problems

What's the matter?
    I have a sore knee.

What's wrong with him?
    His arm hurts.

Let's see.
Cool.
I have to go now.
See you there.

Talking about health

How do you have so much energy?
    I keep fit.
    I exercise every day.
    I take care of my health.

PRONUNCIATION

▶ **A** 🎧 *Listen and repeat.*

/**ow**/

1. n<u>o</u>se	4. b<u>oa</u>t	7. sl<u>ow</u>
2. h<u>o</u>me	5. r<u>oa</u>d	8. yell<u>ow</u>
3. ph<u>o</u>ne	6. s<u>oa</u>p	9. wind<u>ow</u>

▶ **B** 🎧 *Listen and repeat.*

/**ʌ**/

1. f<u>u</u>n	4. d<u>oe</u>s	7. l<u>o</u>ve
2. c<u>u</u>p	5. s<u>o</u>me	8. y<u>ou</u>ng
3. m<u>u</u>ch	6. m<u>o</u>ney	9. m<u>o</u>ther

▶ **C** 🎧 *Listen to each pair of words. Listen again and repeat.*

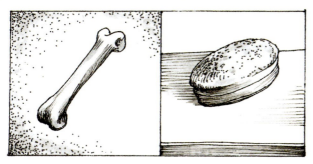

1. a. bone	b. bun		2. a. phone	b. fun

   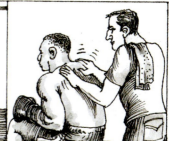

3. a. note	b. nut		4. a. robe	b. rub

 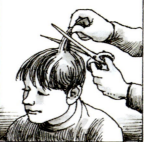 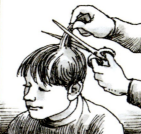 

5. a. coat	b. cut		6. a. boat	b. but

But, Dad...

▶ **D** 🎧 *Look at the words in Part C. Listen and* (circle) *the words you hear.*

▶ **E** 🎧 *Listen and practice.*

1. The y<u>ou</u>ng m<u>o</u>ther is g<u>o</u>ing h<u>o</u>me.
2. R<u>o</u>land's m<u>o</u>ney is <u>u</u>nder the pill<u>ow</u>.
3. Please sh<u>ow</u> <u>u</u>s the yell<u>ow</u> c<u>u</u>ps.
4. D<u>oe</u>s M<u>o</u>na l<u>o</u>ve b<u>o</u>ld colors?
5. N<u>o</u> <u>o</u>ne kn<u>ow</u>s your ph<u>o</u>ne n<u>u</u>mber.
6. J<u>o</u>e's c<u>o</u>mpany is cl<u>o</u>sed on S<u>u</u>ndays.

GRAMMAR SUMMARY

CAN Affirmative

He She I You We They	can	swim.

CAN'T Negative

He She I You We They	can't (cannot)	swim.

Interrogative

Can	he she I you we they	swim?

Short Answers

Yes,	he she I you we they	can.		No,	he she I you we they	can't.

HAVE TO Affirmative

He She	has to	get up early.
I You We They	have to	make breakfast. go to work.

Negative

He She	doesn't (does not)	have to	get up early.
I You We They	don't (do not)		make breakfast. go to work.

Interrogative

Does	he she		get up early?
Do	I you we they	have to	make breakfast? go to work?

Short Answers

Yes,	he she	does.		No,	he she	doesn't.
	I you we they	do.			I you we they	don't.

CONTENTS

Chapter

4

CARTOON STORY

▶ 🎧 *Eddie and his friends are having a party. Listen. Listen and practice.*

QUESTIONS

1. What's happening at Eddie's house tonight?
2. What kind of music are they playing?
3. Why is Mr. Ratcliff upset?
4. Does Mr. Ratcliff complain about the noise? What happens?
5. Do you think it's rude of Mr. Ratcliff to shout at Eddie and Sara?
6. Do you think it's rude to play loud music late at night?
7. Is Eddie surprised when he finds out it's after midnight? What does he say?
8. Do you think Eddie is a good neighbor? Why or why not?
9. How do you get along with your neighbors? What are they like?

GROUP WORK • *Discuss these questions about parties.*

1. Do you like to go to parties? Why or why not?
2. Do you like to give parties? Why or why not?
3. What kind of food and music do you enjoy?
4. What makes a good party? Is it the food, the music or the guests?
5. Are parties in your country different from parties in the United States? How?

Chapter 4   **63**

TOPIC • Special Talents

▶ **WRITING** • *What can these people do well? Write a sentence for each picture using* **can**.

1. <u>She can draw pictures.</u>

2. _____

3. _____

4. _____

▶ **YOUR SPECIAL TALENTS** • *Check (✓) the things you can do well.*

❏ sing   ❏ play the guitar   ❏ draw pictures
❏ dance   ❏ cook   ❏ play soccer
❏ play the piano   ❏ repair things   ❏ play basketball

▶ **PAIR WORK** • *Find out what special talent your partner has.*

A: **What can you do well?**
B: **I can draw pictures.** OR **I can repair things.**

When you discover your partner's special talent, ask more questions such as:

• What do you like to draw?
• When and where do you draw?
• Why do you enjoy drawing?

• Do you take drawing lessons?
• Do you think anyone can learn to draw?
• Can you teach me how to draw?

DECLINING INVITATIONS

▶ 🎧 *Listen. Listen and practice.*

MARVIN: Diana, would you like to see a movie tomorrow?

DIANA: Oh, I'd like to, but I can't. I have to do some work.

MARVIN: Well, maybe some other time.

DIANA: Okay.

▶ **DISCUSSION** • *Diana tells Marvin that she can't go to the movies with him because she has to work. What excuses do you give when you can't or don't want to do something? Do you think it's always necessary to tell the truth?*

▶ **GROUP WORK** • *Discuss the activities in the pictures. When and where do you like to do these things? Which activity is the most popular in your group?*

1

2

3

4

▶ **PAIR WORK** • *Have a conversation like the one above. Student A invites Student B to do something. Student B declines the invitation and gives an excuse.*

▶ **PAIR WORK** • *Ask and answer questions.*

1. A: **Do Lucy and Grover like to dance?**
   B: **Yes, they do.**
   A: **Why?**
   B: **Because it's fun.**

2. A: **Does Mabel like to do housework?**
   B: **No, she doesn't.**
   A: **Why?**
   B: **Because it's boring.**

3. Do people like to eat at Bud's Cafe?

4. Does Carlos want to take a shower?

5. Does Becky want to play basketball?

6. Do Mr. and Mrs. Grand want to visit Canada?

7. Does Nobu have to go to the market?

8. Does Jane have to water the plants?

9. Do Bob and Alice have to go to work today?

GRAMMAR REVIEW

▶ **PAIR WORK** • *Ask and answer questions about the pictures.*

1. money
   A: **Does Roland have much money?**
   B: **Yes, he does. (He has a lot of money.)**
   A: **Does Felix have much money?**
   B: **No, he doesn't.**

2. books
   A: **Does Lulu have many books?**
   B: **No, she doesn't.**
   A: **Does Jane have many books?**
   B: **Yes, she does. (She has a lot of books.)**

3. apples

4. food

5. water

6. chickens

7. customers

8. free time

OCCUPATIONS

▶ 🎧 *Listen. Listen and repeat.* ▶ **WRITING** • *What kind of work do these people do?*

1. Carlos <u>is a mechanic. He repairs</u> <u>cars.</u>

2. Maria and James _____

_____

3. Brenda_____

_____

4. Alan_____

_____

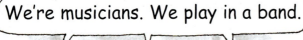

5. Ed and his pals _____

_____

6. Lucy _____

_____

7. Cindy _____

_____

8. Spike and Larry _____

_____

9. Grover _____

_____

10. Kate _____

_____

11. Andy and Mandy _____

_____

12. Mr. Chow _____

_____

▶ **PRACTICE** • *Read out loud the sentences you wrote about the pictures.*

CARTOON STORY

▶ **QUESTIONS**

1. Why does Carlos get upset when the boss asks him to work overtime?
2. What's your opinion of Mr. Hardman? Do you know anyone like him?

LIFE SKILL • Looking for a Job

▶ **WHAT'S HAPPENING?** • *Carlos decides to look for another job. He buys a newspaper and reads the classified ads. Is there a job opening for a mechanic? What does the ad say?*

CLASSIFIED ADS

MECHANIC
Sam's Garage is seeking a full-time mechanic. Mon-Fri. Minimum 5 years experience. Good pay with benefits. Call Vera (470) 756-2104.

NURSING
Mercy Hospital is hiring registered nurses. Four days per week. Spanish is a plus. Excellent salary, benefits. Fax resume (902) 350-6719.

▶ 🎧 *Carlos calls Sam's Garage to ask about their job opening. Listen. Listen and repeat.*

VERA: Sam's Garage. May I help you?

CARLOS: I'm calling about your job opening for a mechanic. Is it still open?

VERA: Yes, it is.

CARLOS: How can I apply for the job?

VERA: You have to come in, get an application, and make an appointment for an interview.

CARLOS: Where are you located?

VERA: 1835 Spring Street.

CARLOS: Thank you. I'll come in tomorrow.

▶ **PAIR WORK** • *Practice the conversation.*

LIFE SKILL • Job Interview

▶ 🎧 *Carlos is having a job interview at Sam's Garage. Listen. Listen and practice.*

MR. BAKER:	Are you Carlos Zapata?
CARLOS:	Yes, sir.
MR. BAKER:	I'm Sam Baker. I'm the owner of this garage.
CARLOS:	Nice to meet you.
MR. BAKER:	So you're applying for a job as a mechanic?
CARLOS:	Yes, sir.
MR. BAKER:	How much experience do you have?
CARLOS:	Five years.
MR. BAKER:	Can you do brakes? Tune-ups?
CARLOS:	Sure. I can do anything you need.
MR. BAKER:	Good. Where are you working now?
CARLOS:	Ace Auto Repair…on Main Street.
MR. BAKER:	I know the place. Why do you want to leave?
CARLOS:	The pay isn't very good. And I don't like the hours. I have to do a lot of overtime.
MR. BAKER:	I see. Do you have any questions for me?
CARLOS:	Yes. How much is the starting salary?
MR. BAKER:	Fifteen dollars an hour.
CARLOS:	Fifteen dollars an hour! That's a lot more than I'm getting now.
MR. BAKER:	It's worth it for a good mechanic. Any more questions?
CARLOS:	No, sir.
MR. BAKER:	Okay, I'll look over your application and call you next week.
CARLOS:	Thank you.

▶ **GROUP WORK** • *Discuss the reasons people quit their jobs. Make a list.*

LIFE SKILL • Job Interview

▶ **JOB INTERVIEW** • *Here are some good questions to ask an employer at a job interview.*

- What are the hours?
- What are my duties?
- How much is the starting salary?
- Do you provide health insurance?

Can you think of more questions to ask when you're at a job interview?

▶ **LOOK AT THE PICTURES** • *The employers are asking job applicants about their skills. Do you have any of these skills? Which ones?*

NATIONAL INSURANCE

Can you type?

Position: Secretary

Olson Travel Agency

Can you speak a foreign language?

Position: Tour Guide

Mario's Pizza Free delivery!

Can you drive a van?

Position: Driver

▶ **PAIR WORK** • *Act out one of the job interviews in the pictures. Feel free to improvise and use your own information.*

EMPLOYER: So you're applying for a job as a _____?

APPLICANT: Yes, I am.

EMPLOYER: How much experience do you have?

APPLICANT: _____.

EMPLOYER: Can you _____?

APPLICANT: _____.

EMPLOYER: Why do you want to leave your present job?

APPLICANT: _____.

EMPLOYER: Do you have any questions?

APPLICANT: Yes. _____?

EMPLOYER: _____.

CARTOON STORY

▶ 🎧 *Listen. Listen and practice.*

▶ **DISCUSSION** • *Do you think Mr. Perkins is a good employee? Why?*

▶ 🎧 *Listen to the story. Check (✓) the words that describe Mr. Perkins.*

1. ☐ grumpy
   ☑ cheerful

2. ☐ on time
   ☐ late

3. ☐ reads the newspaper
   ☐ writes business reports

4. ☐ works fast
   ☐ wastes time

5. ☐ always complains
   ☐ never complains

6. ☐ most popular person
   ☐ very unpopular person

▶ **QUESTIONS**

1. How does Mr. Perkins feel when he comes to work? How can you tell?
2. Do you think Mr. Perkins is well dressed?
3. What kind of reports does Mr. Perkins write? Does he work fast?
4. What does Mr. Perkins say when they give him more work to do?
5. Why does the boss like Mr. Perkins?

▶ **COMPOSITION** • *Write about Mr. Perkins. Begin with this topic sentence:*
<u>Mr. Perkins is a good employee.</u> *Include some details that support the main idea.*

CARTOON STORY

▶ 🎧 *Listen. Listen and practice.*

▶ **DISCUSSION** • *What do you think of Mr. Franken? Give reasons for your opinion.*

▶ **COMPOSITION** • *Write about Mr. Franken. Begin with this topic sentence:*
<u>Mr. Franken is a bad employee.</u> *Include some details that support the main idea.*

VOCABULARY

NOUNS

Work

application form
benefits
client
duties
employer
health insurance
job applicant
job offer
overtime
pay

skills
starting salary
work experience
work habits

Occupations

artist
lawyer
musician
nurse

Other

brakes
math
midnight
nature
noise
rest
tune-up

VERBS

apply
arrest
build
defend
draw
hear
shout

ADJECTIVES

awful
grumpy
popular
rude

ADVERB

again

EXPRESSIONS

Time is money.
So what?
It's worth it.
Maybe some other time.

This report is a mess.
Oh, no…not again.
I can't believe it.
What's happening with you?

Let me see.
Oh, sure.
No problem.
That's better.

I'm working on it.
Where are you located?
Could you turn down the music?
I'd like to, but I can't.

Already?
Isn't this fun?
Are you still on the phone?
Any more questions?

PRONUNCIATION

▶ **A** 🎧 *Listen and repeat.*

/**r**/

1. rich	4. correct	7. story
2. radio	5. tomorrow	8. door
3. room	6. morning	9. letter

▶ **B** 🎧 *Listen and repeat.*

/**l**/

1. late	4. hello	7. call
2. life	5. believe	8. mail
3. love	6. family	9. tell

▶ **C** 🎧 *Listen to each pair of words. Listen again and repeat.*

1. a. fly   b. fry

2. a. glass   b. grass

3. a. light   b. right

4. a. play   b. pray

5. a. climb   b. crime

6. a. collect   b. correct

▶ **D** 🎧 *Look at the words in Part C. Listen and* (circle) *the words you hear.*

▶ **E** 🎧 *Listen and practice.*

1. Lisa is wearing a yellow dress.
2. All of her family is in California.
3. Please call me tomorrow morning.
4. Our school has a wonderful library.
5. There are more apples on the table.
6. Let's play cards in the living room.

TEST

How are you doing?

1. a. I'm doing my job.
   b. Thank you.
   c. Great.
   d. You're welcome.

3. Please wash the dishes.
   They're _____.
   a. clean   c. old
   b. dirty   d. new

5. Mr. Grand is a _____ man.
   He has very little free time.
   a. boring   c. healthy
   b. cheerful   d. busy

7. You can get stamps at the
   _____.
   a. gas station   c. post office
   b. library   d. bank

9. The flower shop is _____ the
   bank and the hotel.
   a. in front of   c. between
   b. behind   d. under

What's Dallas like?

2. a. He's American.
   b. He likes country music.
   c. He would like a new guitar.
   d. He's funny and smart.

4. Lucy isn't working today because
   she's _____.
   a. sick   c. shy
   b. bored   d. rude

6. Amanda is _____. She wants
   a glass of water.
   a. hungry   c. tired
   b. thirsty   d. nervous

8. I'm going to the _____ to
   wash my clothes.
   a. hotel   c. pet shop
   b. market   d. laundromat

10. Carlos and Maria are taking
    a walk _____ the park.
    a. in   c. at
    b. on   d. by

TEST

I have a computer in _____ room.

They're doing _____ homework.

11. a. my   c. his
     b. your   d. her

12. a. his   c. our
     b. her   d. their

13. Those aren't your envelopes.
Don't take _____.

     a. it   c. they
     b. them   d. these

14. Where's your brother? I have
to talk with _____.

     a. he   c. him
     b. her   d. you

15. Sara likes her history class.
_____ it's interesting.

     a. but   c. then
     b. because   d. so

16. Milton doesn't have a car,
_____ he takes the bus to work.

     a. but   c. or
     b. because   d. so

17. Ms. Standfast is sick.
Call a _____.

     a. doctor   c. police officer
     b. mechanic   d. repairman

18. You need an umbrella
on _____ days.

     a. windy   c. rainy
     b. sunny   d. cloudy

_____. We're late
for the concert.

Yes, please.

19. a. Please hurry.
     b. Please relax.
     c. Don't worry.
     d. Take your time.

20. a. Do you take coffee?
     b. Would you like some coffee?
     c. Are you for coffee?
     d. Do you drink some coffee?

21. There's _____ food on the table.
    a. a little   c. much
    b. a lot of   d. many

22. There isn't _____ soup in the pot.
    a. a few   c. much
    b. a little   d. many

23. Hurry up. The show starts

    in _____ minutes.
    a. a few   c. much
    b. a lot of   d. many

24. There aren't _____ people in

    the theater.
    a. some   c. much
    b. no   d. many

25. Betty's coat is ten years old.

    She _____ a new one.
    a. has   c. likes
    b. needs   d. takes

26. We always _____ lunch

    at Mom's Cafe.
    a. eat   c. make
    b. take   d. feed

27. I _____ go to the movies,

    only once or twice a year.
    a. usually   c. sometimes
    b. often   d. hardly ever

28. Listen! Someone _____.
    a. come   c. is coming
    b. comes   d. are coming

29. "Are Jane and Milton working now?"
    "_____."
    a. Yes, they do.
    b. Yes, they are.
    c. No, they aren't.
    d. Not at all.

30. "Does Jane like her job?"
    "_____."
    a. Yes, she like.
    b. No, she don't like.
    c. No, she doesn't.
    d. Yes, she does.

CONTENTS

Chapter

CARTOON STORY

🎧 *Eddie and his friends are talking about their plans for the future. Listen. Listen and practice.*

5. _____

6. _____

7. _____

8. _____

9. _____

10. _____

▶ **PRACTICE** • *Read out loud the sentences you wrote about the pictures.*

GRAMMAR • Future with *be going to*

Negative			
He She	isn't (is not)	going to	watch TV.
They	aren't (are not)		

▶ **WRITING** • *Complete the second sentence below each picture. Use the negative form of* **be going to** *with one of these verbs:* **answer, buy, clean, do, eat, play**.

1. Felix is in a hurry. <u>He isn't going to eat</u> breakfast this morning.

2. Max and Judy are tired. <u>They aren't going to clean</u> their house today.

3. Eddie is busy. _____ _____ basketball this afternoon.

4. Sara has a headache. _____ _____ her homework tonight.

5. The Wongs are having dinner. _____ _____ the phone.

6. Maria doesn't like the pink and green blouse. _____ it.

GRAMMAR • Future with *be going to*

Yes/No Questions			
Is	he she	going to	listen to music? read the newspaper?
Are	they		

Short Answers						
Yes,	he she	is.	No,	he she	isn't.	
	they	are.		they	aren't.	

▶ **PAIR WORK** • *Ask and answer questions about the pictures.*

1. A: **Are Max and Judy going to listen to the radio?**
   B: **No, they aren't. They're going to watch TV.**

2. A: **Is Dallas going to buy some flowers?**
   B: **Yes, he is.**

3. Is Maria going to call her boyfriend?

4. Are Eddie and his friends going to play baseball?

5. Is Suzi going to mail some letters?

6. Is Mr. Denby going to clean the living room?

7. Is Carlos going to wash the car?

8. Are Jason and Lisa going to see a movie?

9. Is Lucy going to wear her green dress?

GRAMMAR • Future with *be going to*

▶ 🎧 *Listen. Listen and repeat.*   ▶ **PAIR WORK 1** • *Practice the conversations.*

What are you going to do after class?

I'm going to play soccer.

What are you going to do tomorrow?

I'm going to clean my garage.

What are you going to do this afternoon?

I'm going to study.

What are you going to do tonight?

I'm going to see my friends.

What are you going to do Friday night?

I'm going dancing.

What are you going to do this weekend?

I'm going to the beach.

▶ **PAIR WORK 2** • *Ask and answer four questions using future time expressions such as **tonight, tomorrow, Friday night, this weekend,** and so on.*

A: **What are you going to do after class?**
B: **I'm going to do my homework.** OR **I'm going to hang out with my friends.**

READINGS

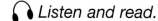 *Listen and read.*

Sara is looking forward to this Friday night. She's going to go to a music concert with her girlfriend. They're going to see Casey and the Cavemen. Sara loves Casey because he's wild and crazy, and he really knows how to play rock 'n' roll. After the show, Sara is going to ask Casey for his autograph. She "can't wait" until Friday night, so she can see her favorite musician in person.

▶ **QUESTIONS**

1. Why is Sara looking forward to Friday night?
2. Who are they going to see?
3. Why does Sara love Casey?
4. What is Sara going to do after the show?

▶ *Listen and read.*

Carlos is looking forward to this weekend. He's going to go camping at Bear Lake with two of his buddies. During the day, they're going to go fishing in the lake. And in the evening, they're going to sit by the fire and tell stories. Carlos loves Bear Lake because it's very quiet and peaceful. It's a wonderful place to relax, enjoy nature, and sleep under the stars.

▶ **QUESTIONS**

1. Why is Carlos looking forward to this weekend?
2. Are they going to go fishing in the lake?
3. What are they going to do in the evening?
4. Why does Carlos love Bear Lake?

▶ **GROUP WORK** • *What are you looking forward to? A day at the beach? A music concert? A basketball game? A party? Discuss your plans and ask each other questions to get the details.*

▶ **COMPOSITION** • *Write a paragraph about something special or fun that you're looking forward to. Include some details.*

▶ **CLASS ACTIVITY** • *Look at the picture. What do you think John and Mary are talking about? What do you think John wants to do?*

▶ 🎧 *Listen. Listen and repeat.*

JOHN: Guess what! I'm going to buy a piano next month.

MARY: How exciting! What kind of piano are you going to buy?

JOHN: An upright piano. A grand piano is too expensive.

MARY: How much does an upright piano cost?

JOHN: A new one costs several thousand dollars.

MARY: That's not cheap.

JOHN: I know. I hope to find a good used piano for two thousand.

MARY: Do you know how to play?

JOHN: No. I'm going to take lessons. I need to find a teacher.

MARY: What kind of music would you like to play?

JOHN: You aren't going to believe this, but I want to play jazz!

MARY: You can do it!

▶ **THINK ABOUT IT** • *In the conversation above, John tells Mary that he's going to buy a piano. What questions does Mary ask in order to get more information? Find Mary's questions and underline them. Then read the questions out loud.*

GRAMMAR • Verb + Infinitive

I	want to hope to plan to	take a vacation.

I'd like to	go to Texas. stay on a ranch. ride horses.

▶ 🎧 **WRITING** • *Listen to the people in the pictures as they talk about their plans, hopes, and desires. Think of three questions to ask each person. Write questions that begin with* **Who, What, Where, Why,** *and* **How.**

I plan to take my vacation next month.

1. <u>Where do you plan to go?</u>
2. <u>Why do you want to go there?</u>
3. <u>Who are you going to go with?</u>

I hope to buy a house next year.

1. _____
2. _____
3. _____

I'd like to change jobs.

1. _____
2. _____
3. _____

I don't want to live here anymore.

1. _____
2. _____
3. _____

▶ **PAIR WORK** • *Choose one of the situations above and write a dialogue that includes at least three questions. Act out the conversation before the class.*

▶ 🎧 *Milton is shopping for a leather jacket. Listen. Listen and practice.*

▶ **PRICES** • *How much do these items cost? Write down the average price.*

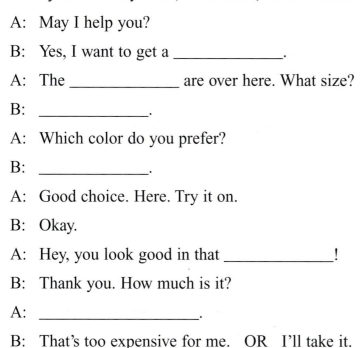

1. a leather jacket _____

2. a sweater _____

3. a t-shirt _____

▶ **PAIR WORK** • *Act out a conversation similar to the conversation on pages 92-93. Student A is the salesperson and Student B is the customer. The customer wants to buy a leather jacket, a sweater, or a t-shirt.*

A: May I help you?

B: Yes, I want to get a _____.

A: The _____ are over here. What size?

B: _____.

A: Which color do you prefer?

B: _____.

A: Good choice. Here. Try it on.

B: Okay.

A: Hey, you look good in that _____!

B: Thank you. How much is it?

A: _____.

B: That's too expensive for me.   OR   I'll take it.

SIZES

small medium large

COLORS

- red
- orange
- yellow
- green
- blue
- purple
- beige
- brown
- black
- gray
- white
- pink

DESCRIBING PEOPLE • Personality

▶ **WRITING** • *The pictures below show different people and their personalities. Choose one sentence from the box that explains the "character adjective" for each person.*

> …likes to give people presents.
> …is afraid she will fail the test.
> …always smiles and says "hello."
> …gets angry a lot.
> …doesn't think about other people.
> …doesn't get upset if things go wrong.
> …is afraid to talk with new people.
> …is sure she will do well on the test.

1. Carol is outgoing. <u>She always smiles and says "hello."</u>

2. Janet is shy. _____

_____

3. Dan is generous. _____

_____

4. Frank is selfish. _____

_____

5. Alicia is confident. _____

6. Carmen is nervous. _____

_____

_____

No problem.

7. Mr. Mayberry is easygoing. _____

8. Mr. Stonewall is bad-tempered. _____

_____

_____

▶ **DISCUSSION**

1. Are you outgoing? How do you show it?
2. When do you feel shy? Give an example.
3. How can you be generous without giving money or presents?
4. Do you know any selfish people? How do they show it?
5. Would you like to be more confident? What would you like to do better?
6. What makes you nervous? Give an example.
7. Are you easygoing? How do you act when things go wrong?
8. Do you know anyone who is bad-tempered? How does he or she show it?

▶ **PAIR WORK** • *Ask each other the same questions. Write down three things that you learned about your partner. Then tell the class.*

CHARACTER SKETCH

MS. KROCK

 Look and listen.

- Who is Ms. Krock talking to?
- What is she saying?
- How does her secretary feel?
- What's your opinion of Ms. Krock?
- Do you have some advice for Ms. Krock?

 Listen and read.

Ms. Krock is the president of her own company – Krock Insurance. She has three employees, and she loves to give them orders. Ms. Krock is a mean boss. She gives her employees too much work, and she yells at them when they don't finish their work on time. Everyone in the office is stressed out, but Ms. Krock doesn't care. She gives her employees only five minutes for their coffee break, and they have to pay for the coffee. Obviously, it isn't much fun to work for Ms. Krock.

THINK ABOUT IT • *What's the main idea of the paragraph? Give some examples of Ms. Krock's behavior that support the main idea.*

BRUNO

 Look and listen.

- What is Bruno thinking about – his homework or the girl?
- Why doesn't he talk to her?
- What's your opinion of Bruno?
- Do you have some advice for Bruno?

 Listen and read.

Bruno is a college student. He's doing well in school, but he doesn't have a very good social life. Bruno spends most of his time studying at the college library. He hardly ever goes to parties or other social events. He doesn't feel comfortable when he's around a lot of people. Bruno is very shy. When he sees a cute girl at the library, he's afraid to talk to her. He just sits there in silence. It's a shame, because Bruno is a great guy. All he needs is a little confidence.

THINK ABOUT IT • *What's the main idea of the paragraph? Give some examples of Bruno's behavior that support the main idea.*

WRITING A CHARACTER SKETCH

PAIR WORK • *Pretend you're sitting in the Magnolia Restaurant. You see a large, well-dressed man at the next table. His name is Mr. Wiley. Observe him for a moment. Then discuss your observations with your partner. What is your opinion of Mr. Wiley?*

QUESTIONS • *If you aren't sure, try to guess the answers. Use your imagination.*

1. What does Mr. Wiley do for a living?
2. Does he work near the Magnolia Restaurant?
3. How often does he go there for lunch?
4. Are the employees happy to see Mr. Wiley when he comes to the restaurant?
5. What kind of personality does Mr. Wiley have?
6. Does he really enjoy being with people?
7. Does Mr. Wiley like to tell sad stories and make people cry?
8. Does he think life is wonderful or miserable?
9. Does he make the most of every moment?

CLUSTERING • *Add as many ideas as possible to the cluster. Write down everything you can think of about Mr. Wiley – everything you can see, feel or imagine.*

COMPOSITION 1 • *Look over the details in your cluster. What kind of person is Mr. Wiley? Write a paragraph that describes his character and personality. Include some details that support your opinion. For ideas, look at the picture, the questions, and the details in the cluster. Use the paragraphs about Bruno and Ms. Krock as models.*

GROUP WORK • *Take turns telling the group about an interesting person you know. Use a character adjective (generous, selfish, funny, bad-tempered), to describe this person. The other students in the group ask questions to get more information.*

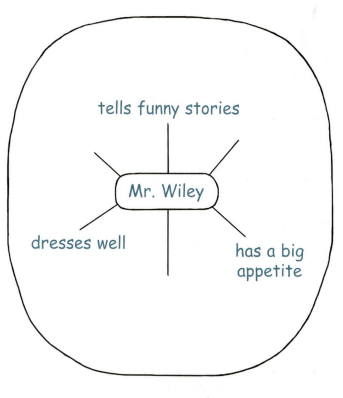

COMPOSITION 2 • *Write a character sketch about someone you know.*

VOCABULARY

NOUNS

advice
air force
autograph
biology
buddies
camel
coffee break
community college
confidence
degree
impression
leather jacket
orders
physical eduction
rock 'n' roll
several

silence
social event
stories
thousand

VERBS

camp
change
fish
mail
plan
yell

ADJECTIVES

shy ≠ outgoing
generous ≠ selfish
nervous ≠ confident
easygoing ≠ bad-tempered
gentle ≠ mean
wonderful ≠ miserable
new ≠ used
wild

ADVERBS

anymore
obviously

EXPRESSIONS

Shopping for clothes

What size?
   Medium.
Which color do you prefer?
   I like brown.

Here. Try it on.
   Okay.
Hey, you look good in that jacket.
   You really think so?

She doesn't care.
She can't wait.
It's a shame.

He's a great guy.
He's looking forward to this weekend.
He makes the most of every moment.

Guess what!
I'd like to change jobs.
You can do it.

It's cheaper that way.
Hey, that's a great idea!
How exciting!

PRONUNCIATION

A 🎧 *Listen and repeat.*

/**f**/

1. face	4. phone	7. safe
2. food	5. office	8. wife
3. five	6. careful	9. laugh

B 🎧 *Listen and repeat.*

/**v**/

1. vase	4. every	7. love
2. vine	5. movie	8. save
3. very	6. seven	9. leave

C 🎧 *Listen to each pair of words. Listen again and repeat.*

1. a. face   b. vase

2. a. fine   b. vine

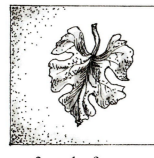

3. a. leaf   b. leave

4. a. half   b. have

5. a. life   b. live

6. a. surf   b. serve

D 🎧 *Look at the words in Part C. Listen and* (circle) *the words you hear.*

E 🎧 *Listen and practice.*

1. The leaves are falling from the vine.
2. I never leave the office before five.
3. My lovely wife has a beautiful voice.
4. We often have visitors on Friday.
5. We love to laugh and have fun.
6. French movies are very funny.

GRAMMAR SUMMARY

BE GOING TO Affirmative

He She	's (is)		see a movie.
I	'm (am)	going to	listen to music.
You We They	're (are)		play tennis.

Negative

He She	isn't (is not)		see a movie.
I	'm not (am not)	going to	listen to music.
You We They	aren't (are not)		play tennis.

Interrogative

Is	he she		see a movie?
Am	I	going to	listen to music?
Are	you we they		play tennis?

Short Answers

	he she	is.
Yes,	I	am.
	you we they	are.

	he she	isn't.
No,	I	'm not.
	you we they	aren't.

Questions with WHO, WHAT, WHEN, WHERE

Who		Jane going to visit?	Her brother.
What	's (is)	Mike going to buy?	A computer.
When		Lucy going to have lunch?	At one o'clock.
Where		Bob going to park his car?	In the street.

VERB + INFINITIVE

	want to	
I	hope to	take my next vacation in Mexico.
	plan to	

CONTENTS

▶ **TOPICS**

Vacations

Saving money

▶ **GRAMMAR**

Past tense of *to be*

Possessive pronouns

▶ **FUNCTIONS**

Talking about the past

Identifying possessions

Agreeing and disagreeing

▶ **WRITING PROCESS**

Unity

Adding interesting details

Deleting unnecessary details

▶ **COMPOSITION**

Describing a scene

▶ **PRONUNCIATION**

/ɛr/ vs. /ɔr/

Chapter

6

CARTOON STORY

▶ 🎧 *It's Tuesday morning at Grant Elementary School. Listen. Listen and practice.*

Ms. Blake's class started at 8:30 this morning.

Nancy and Peter **were** on time. They **weren't** late.

Dennis **was** late. He **wasn't** on time.

The students **were** bored because the lesson today **wasn't** very interesting.

Ms. Blake **was** disappointed because the students **weren't** interested in the lesson.

▶ **QUESTIONS**

1. Were Nancy and Peter on time to Ms. Blake's class?
2. Why was Ms. Blake upset with Dennis?
3. Why were the students bored?
4. Why was Ms. Blake disappointed?

GRAMMAR • Past tense of *to be*

Affirmative		
I He She It	was	early.
		on time.
You We They	were	late.

Negative		
I He She It	wasn't (was not)	early.
		on time.
You We They	weren't (were not)	late.

▶ **WRITING** • *Complete the sentences using* **was, wasn't, were, weren't.**
After you finish, read the sentences out loud.

1. The weather __was__ nice yesterday, but there __weren't__ many people at the beach.

2. Max and Judy _____ worried because there _____ much gas in the car.

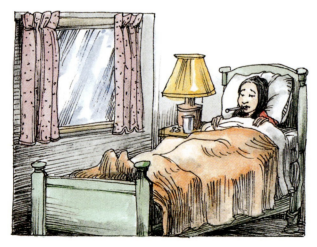

3. Mary _____ at work last week because she _____ sick.

4. The avocados _____ very large, but they _____ expensive.

5. Joe _____ very busy yesterday. There _____ many customers at the cafe.

6. Annabelle _____ disappointed with the photos. They _____ very good.

7. There _____ some cute dolls in the window, but Josie _____ interested.

8. Mario _____ happy. The jacket _____ too big, and the pants _____ too small.

9. Lucy and Grover _____ at home last night. They _____ at the movies.

10. Everyone _____ bored at the last meeting. The speaker _____ very interesting.

GRAMMAR • Past tense of *to be*

Yes/No Questions		
Was	he she it	early? on time?
Were	you they	late?

Short Answers					
Yes,	he she it	was.	No,	he she it	wasn't.
	you they	were.		you they	weren't.

▶ **PAIR WORK** • *Ask and answer questions about the pictures.*

1. A: **Was Maria awake at six o'clock?**
   B: **No, she wasn't. She was asleep.**

2. A: **Were Max and Judy at home last night?**
   B: **Yes, they were.**

3. A: **Was the weather sunny yesterday?**
   B: **No, it wasn't. It was cloudy.**

4. Was Amos stressed out this morning?

5. Was the food good at Mom's Cafe?

6. Were Linda and Billy on time to class?

7. Was last Sunday a good day for a picnic?

8. Were Lucy and Grover busy this morning?

9. Was Suzi happy yesterday?

GRAMMAR • Possessive Pronouns

▶ 🎧 *Listen. Listen and repeat.*

POSSESSIVE PRONOUNS		
Whose dog is that?	It's	mine. yours. his. hers. ours. theirs.

▶ 🎧 *Listen. Listen and repeat.* ▶ **PAIR WORK** • *Practice the conversations.*

▶ **WRITING** • *Complete the conversations using these words:*

this that these those	mine yours his hers ours theirs

Whose motorcycle is <u>that</u>?

It's <u>hers</u>.

Whose chocolates are <u>these</u>?

They're <u>ours</u>.

Whose books are _____?

They're ____.

Whose ball is _____?

It's _____.

Whose hat is _____?

It's _____.

Whose envelopes are _____?

They're _____.

TOPIC • Vacations

🎧 *The Ratcliffs are making plans for their summer vacation. Listen. Listen and practice.*

QUESTIONS

1. Where would Mrs. Ratcliff like to go for her summer vacation?
2. Does Mr. Ratcliff agree with his wife? What does he say?
3. Where does their son, Junior, want to go?
4. Does Mr. Ratcliff agree with Junior? What does he say?
5. Does Mrs. Ratcliff want to go camping? Why or why not?

DISCUSSION • *What are some good places to take a vacation in your country? Why are these places popular?*

GROUP WORK • *Pretend that your group is going on vacation next month. Where would you like to go? Choose a destination and tell the class.*

TOPIC • Saving Money

▶ **THINK ABOUT IT** • *There are many ways you can save money. Look at the ideas in the box and write an appropriate sentence below each picture. After you finish, read the sentences out loud.*

> buy things on sale   do your own repairs   get your haircuts at home
> ride a bicycle to work   eat by candlelight   plant a vegetable garden

1. <u>You can do your own repairs.</u>

2. _____

3. _____

4. _____

5. _____

6. _____

▶ **GROUP WORK** • *Think of some other ways you can save money. Make a list and share your ideas with the class.*

UNITY

A *Look at the picture. What's the main idea? Describe some details.*

B *There is one detail that doesn't belong in the picture. Write it on this line:*

_____

We know that paragraphs are like pictures; they both have main ideas and details. Good paragraphs contain only the details that tell more about the main idea. This gives the paragraph **unity**.

C *Read the paragraph below and underline the main idea.*

Summer is my favorite time of the year. I love to go to the beach on summer days when the weather is warm and sunny. I also enjoy rock music. Another reason I like summer is that the days are long; there's more time to relax and have fun. Maybe it's just my imagination, but people seem to be happier during the summer. I know I feel that way.

There is one sentence in the paragraph that isn't related to the main idea. Which sentence is it? If you chose "I also enjoy rock music," you're right. The fact that the writer enjoys rock music is not directly related to the main idea of the paragraph. The main idea is that summer is the writer's favorite time of the year. Which details in the paragraph tell more about the main idea?

DELETING UNNECESSARY DETAILS

▶ **D** *There is an unnecessary detail in each of the following paragraphs. Draw a line through the one sentence in each paragraph that isn't related to the main idea.*

1.   Susie wants to be a fashion designer when she grows up. She loves to look at her mother's fashion magazines and learn about all the latest styles. She thinks that watching TV is a lot of fun, too. Susie spends many hours drawing pictures of the beautiful clothes she would like to make. The dresses always have bright colors and look very elegant. Although she's only ten years old, Susie already has a style of her own.

2.   I have wonderful neighbors. I can always count on them if I need a favor. For example, the people next door are always happy to take care of my dog when I go on vacation. My dog sleeps on the porch. Another reason I like my neighbors is that they take pride in their homes. On the weekend, I often see them planting flowers, cutting the grass, and so on. That's what makes our street beautiful. I'm very lucky to have such good neighbors.

3.   Mary loves to go window shopping at the mall. It's a huge place with more than one hundred shops and three department stores. You can find almost anything there, even toy bears that sing. Once in a while, Mary buys something when she goes to the mall. But most of the time, she just wants to look around and see what's new in the stores. She has a lot of free time on the weekend. Window shopping at the mall is a great way for Mary to relax and have fun.

ADDING INTERESTING DETAILS

▶ **WHAT'S GOING ON?** • *Look at the picture. What's the main idea?*

Here's a short description of the picture. The first sentence states the main idea.

> Sandra and Luis are having a disagreement. Sandra wants to stop and look at some hats in the window. But Luis isn't interested in window shopping. He wants to see the new Tarzan movie.

This paragraph isn't very interesting because it lacks details. Details are necessary to make writing come to life. A good way to find details is to ask questions. So ask questions whenever you write a composition.

▶ **ADDING DETAILS** • *Let's discuss the questions below and see if we can find some details that will make the original paragraph more interesting.*

1. Where are Sandra and Luis?
2. Why is Sandra pointing to one of the hats in the window?
3. What does the hat look like?
4. How does Luis feel about window shopping? Why?
5. Do you think Sandra and Luis enjoy the same things?
6. Why does Luis want to see the new Tarzan movie?
7. Why doesn't Sandra want to see Tarzan?
8. What kind of movies do you think Sandra likes?

ADDING INTERESTING DETAILS

▶ **PAIR WORK** • *Find a partner and discuss the picture on page 114. Make a list of four details that aren't in the short description of the picture. When you finish, read your list to the class.*

Example: <u>Sandra is pointing to a green hat with a big red feather.</u>

1. _____

2. _____

3. _____

4. _____

Here's a new paragraph about the picture.

    Sandra and Luis are having a disagreement. Sandra wants to stop and look at some hats in the window. She's pointing to a green hat with a big red feather. She thinks it's funny-looking. Luis isn't interested in window shopping. He thinks it's boring to look at hats and dresses. He wants to see the new Tarzan movie. Tarzan is strong and brave, and he has a lot of exciting adventures. Luis would like to be like Tarzan.

You can see that the new paragraph is much better than the first one. It gives a better idea of what's happening in the picture. What details can you find in the second paragraph that aren't in the first paragraph?

▶ 🎧 **WRITING A SCENE** • *We can change the second paragraph into a scene by giving Sandra and Luis some dialogue. Dialogue is another way of providing details that make a paragraph more interesting. Listen to what Sandra and Luis are saying.*

    "Luis, look at that hat!" says Sandra, pointing to a green hat with a big red feather. "Isn't it wild?"

    Luis is looking in the direction of the Plaza Theater. "Come on, Sandra! Let's go and see the new Tarzan movie."

    Sandra rolls her eyes. "Are you sure you want to see Tarzan?"

    "You bet," says Luis. "Tarzan is cool."

▶ 🎧 **ROLE PLAY** • *Listen to the conversation again. Then role play with a partner. Add your own ideas.*

DESCRIBING A SCENE

▶ **A** 🎧 *Look and listen.*

▶ **B** *Discuss these questions with your teacher.*

- Why is Melinda nervous?
- Who is in the audience?
- How well is Melinda playing?
- What is the reaction of the audience?

▶ **C** *Read the paragraph about the picture.*

    Melinda Lee's piano recital isn't going well. Melinda is very nervous.
(1) _____. She wants to play
well for her parents. She also wants to impress her teacher, Mr. Flounder.
Melinda is playing *Twinkle, Twinkle, Little Star*. It's her favorite song, but she's
making a lot of mistakes. Mr. and Mrs. Lee want to encourage their daughter.
(2) _____. Everyone else in the audience
is silent. (3) _____. Mr. Flounder is surprised
that Melinda is playing badly. (4) _____.

▶ **D** *Add these details to make the paragraph more interesting.*

> They're smiling and clapping loudly.
> She's one of his best students.
> This is her first piano recital.
> They feel sorry for Melinda.

DESCRIBING A SCENE

▶ **WHAT'S GOING ON?** • *Look at the picture. What is the mailman's problem? What do you think the mailman and Charlie are saying to each other?*

▶ 🎧 *Listen to the conversation.*

▶ **KEY WORDS**

mean bulldog	mailman	come	laugh	be afraid of
sharp teeth	bills	deliver	leave	get scared
bad attitude	house	growl	hate	feel sorry for
	porch	run away	pay	be glad

▶ **QUESTIONS** • *If you aren't sure of the answers, use your imagination.*

1. Why does the mailman hate to come to Charlie's house?
2. Does the mailman usually have some bills for Charlie?
3. Why can't the mailman deliver the bills?
4. Why is the mailman afraid of the dog?
5. What happens when the dog growls at the mailman?
6. Does Charlie feel sorry for the mailman?
7. Why is Charlie glad when the mailman leaves?
8. What kind of person is Charlie?

▶ **STORYTELLING** • *Write a short story about the picture. Use the picture, the key words, and the questions for ideas. Include a line or two of dialogue if you wish. Begin with this topic sentence:* <u>The mailman hates to come to Charlie's house.</u>

VOCABULARY

NOUNS

attitude
audience
bear
candlelight
chocolates
disagreement
doll
fashion designer
feather
grass

imagination
mistakes
repairs
reaction
reason
recital
speaker
style
window-shopping
yesterday

VERBS

contain
cut
deliver
encourage
growl
grow up
run away
seem

ADJECTIVES

asleep
awake
brave
huge
latest
sharp
surprised
unnecessary

ADVERBS

badly
probably

POSSESSIVE PRONOUNS

| mine | his | ours |
| yours | hers | theirs |

EXPRESSIONS

He has a bad attitude.
He doesn't feel sorry for the mailman.

Nancy was on time.
So was Peter.

I can always count on my neighbors.
They take pride in their homes.

So can you.
You bet.

People seem to be happier.
I know I feel that way.

Me, too.
You see?

It's too expensive.
We can't afford it.

For example…
…and so on.

PRONUNCIATION

▶ **A** 🎧 *Listen and repeat.*

/ɛr/

1. care
2. fare
3. stare
4. fair
5. pair
6. chair
7. bear
8. wear
9. their

▶ **B** 🎧 *Listen and repeat.*

/ɔr/

1. more
2. store
3. corn
4. door
5. floor
6. porch
7. four
8. short
9. reports

▶ **C** 🎧 *Listen to each pair of words. Listen again and repeat.*

1. a. scare   b. score

2. a. pear   b. pour

3. a. stare   b. store

4. a. chairs   b. chores

5. a. fair   b. four

6. a. mare   b. more

▶ **D** 🎧 *Look at the words in Part C. Listen and (circle) the words you hear.*

▶ **E** 🎧 *Listen and practice.*

1. I'm scared of the bear over there.
2. No more popcorn for Boris.
3. I'm wearing my air force uniform.
4. Mary and Norm don't care for New York.
5. There are four chairs on the porch.
6. Larry can repair the door in the morning.

GRAMMAR SUMMARY

Past of *to be* Affirmative

I He She It	was	early.
		on time.
You We They	were	late.

Negative

I He She It	wasn't (was not)	early.
		on time.
You We They	weren't (were not)	late.

Interrogative

Was	I he she it	early?
		on time?
Were	you we they	late?

Short Answers

Yes,	I he she it	was.
	you we they	were.

No,	I he she it	wasn't.
	you we they	weren't.

POSSESSIVE PRONOUNS

Whose dog is that?	It's	mine. yours. his. hers. ours. theirs.

CONTENTS

▶ **TOPICS**

Daily routines

The weekend

Personal experiences

▶ **GRAMMAR**

Simple past tense

▶ **FUNCTIONS**

Talking about past actions

Telling a story

Showing interest

Taking a message

Reporting an emergency

▶ **COMPOSITION**

Writing about personal experiences

▶ **PRONUNCIATION**

Verbs: different sounds for the *–ed* ending

CARTOON STORY

Roger and Felix work at the same office. Listen. Listen and practice.

▶ **A** 🎧 *Here are nine simple past verbs in the cartoon story. Listen and repeat.*

got	made	bought	left	took	ate	went	read	had

▶ **B** *Write the past tense of the verbs below. Then read each pair of verbs aloud.*

1. buy <u>bought</u>
2. eat _____
3. get _____

4. go _____
5. have _____
6. leave _____

7. make _____
8. read _____
9. take _____

GRAMMAR • Simple Past Tense

▶ 🎧 *Listen. Listen and repeat.*

1. Yesterday John **got up** at six o'clock.

2. He **ate** bacon and eggs for breakfast.

3. He **left** the house at seven.

4. He **took** the bus to work.

5. He **had** lunch at the office.

6. He **came** home at five-thirty.

7. He **made** soup for dinner.

8. He **read** a book after dinner.

9. He **went** to bed at ten-thirty.

▶ **PRACTICE** • *Answer the teacher; then ask each other questions about John.*

1. When did John get up yesterday?
2. What did he eat for breakfast?
3. When did he leave the house?
4. How did he get to work?
5. Where did he have lunch?
6. When did he come home?
7. What did he make for dinner?
8. What did he do after dinner?
9. When did he go to bed?

▶ **PAIR WORK** • *Ask and answer the same questions about Jane on page 125.*

A: **When did Jane get up yesterday?**
B: **She got up at six-thirty.**

GRAMMAR • Simple Past Tense

🎧 *Listen. Listen and repeat.*

A: **Did Jane get up at six-thirty?**
B: **Yes, she did.**

A: **Did Jane leave the house at eight o'clock?**
B: **No, she didn't. (She left at seven-thirty.)**

A: **Did she eat cereal for breakfast?**
B: **Yes, she did.**

A: **Did she walk to work?**
B: **No, she didn't. (She took the bus.)**

▶ **PRACTICE** • *Answer the teacher; then ask each other questions about Jane.*

1. Did Jane get up at six o'clock?
2. Did she eat cereal for breakfast?
3. Did she leave the house at seven-thirty?
4. Did she walk to work?
5. Did she have lunch at the office?

6. Did she come home at six o'clock?
7. Did she make soup for dinner?
8. Did she read the newspaper after dinner?
9. Did she go to bed at ten-thirty?

▶ **PAIR WORK** • *Ask and answer the same questions about John on page 124.*

A: **Did John get up at six o'clock?**
B: **Yes, he did.**

A: **Did he eat cereal for breakfast?**
B: **No, he didn't. He ate bacon and eggs.**

GRAMMAR • Simple Past Tense

Wh- Questions			
When			get up?
What	did	you	eat for breakfast?
How			get to work?
Where			go after work?

Affirmative	
	got up at six o'clock.
	ate a bowl of cereal.
I	drove to work.
	went home after work.

▶ **WRITING** • *Answer the following questions about yourself.*

1. How did you get to school/work yesterday? I walked.   OR   I took the bus.

2. Where did you go after school/work?_____

3. What did you have for dinner last night? _____

4. When did you go to bed? _____

5. When did you get up this morning? _____

6. What did you eat for breakfast? _____

▶ **PAIR WORK** • *Ask and answer the questions above.*

A: **How did you get to work yesterday?**
B: **I drove to work.**   OR   **I took the bus.**   OR   **I walked.**

Yes/No Questions		
		get up early yesterday?
Did	you	eat a big breakfast?
		get to work on time?
		go home after work?

Short Answers					
Yes,	I	did.	No,	I	didn't.

▶ **WRITING** • *Answer the following questions about yourself.*

1. Did you study last night? Yes, I did.   OR   No, I didn't.

2. Did you go to bed late?_____

3. Did you get up early this morning? _____

4. Did you have a big breakfast? _____

5. Did you leave the house in a hurry? _____

6. Did you get to school/work on time? _____

▶ **PAIR WORK** • *Ask and answer the questions above.*

A: **Did you study last night?**
B: **Yes, I did.**   OR   **No, I didn't.**

GRAMMAR • Simple Past Tense

▶ 🎧 *Listen. Listen and repeat.*

Yesterday Maria **went** to the store and **bought** some groceries. She **got** some strawberries that **were** on sale.

This morning the girls **went** to the park and **played** soccer. A lot of people **watched** the game.

Last Friday, Dallas and Daisy **went** to a movie. They **saw** a new comedy called *Big Deal*.

Last night, Lucy and Grover **stayed** home. Lucy **read** a book, and Grover **listened to** some CDs.

SIMPLE PAST	Regular Verbs
listen - listened	talk - talked
play - played	walk - walked
stay - stayed	watch - watched
study - studied	work - worked

Regular verbs end in **-ed**.

SIMPLE PAST	Irregular Verbs	
buy - bought	get - got	make - made
come - came	go - went	read - read
do - did	have - had	see - saw
eat - ate	leave - left	take - took

For a list of irregular verbs, see the Appendix.

▶ **PAIR WORK** • *Ask and answer questions. Use past time expressions like* **yesterday, yesterday afternoon, last night, this morning, last Saturday.**

A: **What did you do yesterday afternoon?**

B: **I took a walk in the park. What about you?**

A: **I stayed home and studied for my history test.**

GRAMMAR • Simple Past Tense

What	did	he she they	do last night?

He She They	went to a movie.

Irregular:
buy - bought
meet - met
wear - wore

▶ 🎧 *Listen. Listen and repeat.*

▶ **PAIR WORK** • *Practice the conversations.*

▶ **WRITING** • *Fill in the answers. Then read the conversations aloud.*

1. What did Maria wear to the party?
   She wore a red dress.

2. Who did Carlos dance with?

3. When did Daisy go to bed last night?

4. How did Milton go to work this morning?

What did Pete and Fred have for lunch?

Where did the girls play soccer?

Who did Dallas call last night?

What did Jane buy at the supermarket?

Where did Ken and Suzi meet after school?

GRAMMAR • Simple Past Tense

Negative						
He She	didn't (did not)	buy anything	because	he she	didn't (did not)	have any money.

▶ **WRITING** • *Complete the sentences about the pictures using the negative form of these verbs:* **answer, finish, go, have, open, talk**. *Use each verb only once.*

1. Maria ___didn't finish___ the housework.

2. Grover _____ the phone.

3. Felix _____ breakfast.

4. Suzi _____ to her boyfriend.

5. Jimmy _____ to school.

6. Natasha _____ the door.

▶ **PAIR WORK** • *Ask and answer questions.*

A: **Why didn't Maria finish the housework?**
B: **Because she was tired.**

Word Bank		
afraid	busy	sick
angry	in a hurry	✓tired

GRAMMAR • Simple Past Tense

Yes/No Question		
Did	he she they	go to a movie?

Short Answers					
Yes,	he she they	did.	No,	he she they	didn't.

▶ **PAIR WORK** • *Ask and answer questions about the pictures.*

1. A: **Did Jack and Jill have a good time at the party?**
   B: **Yes, they did.**

2. A: **Did Felix win the checkers game?**
   B: **No, he didn't. He lost.**

3. Did Suzi listen to music last night?

4. Did the girls play soccer yesterday?

5. Did Milton drive to work this morning?

6. Did Jane leave the office in a hurry?

7. Did Grover and Lucy stay home last night?

8. Did Jason write a letter to his girlfriend?

9. Did Anna study after school?

CONVERSATION • Getting the Details

▶ 🎧 *Listen. Listen and practice.*

MARY: Hi, Lisa. How was your weekend?

LISA: Great! I went hiking on Sunday.

MARY: Where did you go?

LISA: Mount Pleasant. We climbed all the way to the top.

MARY: That's a beautiful place! Who did you go with?

LISA: My boyfriend, Jason.

MARY: Did you take your camera?

LISA: Yeah, we got some great pictures.

▶ **THINK ABOUT IT** • *Lisa told Mary that she went hiking on Sunday. What questions did Mary ask to get more information?*

▶ 🎧 **WRITING** • *In the next conversation, Eddie tells Mr. Hill that he played basketball on Saturday. Mr. Hill asks Eddie some questions to get the details. Listen to the conversation. Then complete Mr. Hill's questions.*

MR. HILL: What did you do last weekend, Eddie?

EDDIE: I played basketball. We had a big game Saturday.

MR. HILL: Who _____?

EDDIE: My team won. The score was 67 to 65.

MR. HILL: Hey, that was a close game! How many _____?

EDDIE: I made 12 points.

MR. HILL: Not bad. When _____?

EDDIE: Our next game is this Sunday. Do you want to come?

MR. HILL: Sure. That'll be great.

▶ **PAIR WORK** • *Practice the conversation.*

CONVERSATION • Getting the Details

Which beach did you go to?	Was it expensive?	What was it about?
✓ Did you buy anything?	Who was in it?	Did you meet anyone interesting?
What movie did you see?	How was the weather?	When are you going to wear it?
Where was the party?	Who was there?	Did you go in the water?

▶ 🎧 **WRITING** • *Look at the pictures and listen to the conversations. Then read the questions in the box. Write the three best questions for each picture.*

1. <u>Did you buy anything?</u>
2. _____
3. _____

1. _____
2. _____
3. _____

1. _____
2. _____
3. _____

1. _____
2. _____
3. _____

▶ **GROUP WORK** • *Think of more questions for each picture. What do you want to know more about? Write as many questions as possible in five minutes.*

▶ **PAIR WORK 1** • *Improvise a conversation about each picture.*

▶ **PAIR WORK 2** • *Ask about your partner's weekend. Try to get the details.*

THE BIG GAME

▶ 🎧 *What happened in the last minute of the big game yesterday between the Tigers and the Wildcats? Listen as Jeff Grady, a player for the Wildcats, describes the action. "The score was tied 65 to 65 and the Tigers had the ball…"*

▶ **STORYTELLING** • *Look at the pictures and put the sentences in the right order.*

____ The ball went through the hoop.

____ The coach sent me into the game.

____ I was a hero.

____ A player from the other team came at me.

____ Suddenly, he fell and hurt his leg.

____ I shot the ball.

_1_ Our best player stole the ball from the Tigers.

____ One of my teammates passed me the ball.

____ Everyone cheered.

Irregular:
come - came
fall - fell
go - went
hurt - hurt
send - sent
shoot - shot
steal - stole

PICTURE STORY

▶ **WHAT'S GOING ON?** • *Look at the pictures. What's happening?*

▶ 🎧 **DICTATION** • *Josie Morales is from Mexico. Listen as Josie describes her first day at school in America. Listen again and write each sentence, line by line.*

_____

_____

_____

_____

_____

_____

_____

_____

_____

_____

_____

🎧 *Listen to the story about the mailman, the bulldog, and Charlie Barnum. Listen again and check (✓) the key words you hear in the story.*

1. ☐ fireman
   ☑ mailman

2. ☐ experience
   ☐ problem

3. ☐ deliver
   ☐ send

4. ☐ postcards
   ☐ bills

5. ☐ through
   ☐ around

6. ☐ door
   ☐ gate

7. ☐ meeting
   ☐ greeting

8. ☐ mean
   ☐ clean

9. ☐ strong
   ☐ sharp

10. ☐ attitude
    ☐ personality

11. ☐ growled
    ☐ yelled

12. ☐ tired
    ☐ scared

13. ☐ dropped
    ☐ lost

14. ☐ ran away
    ☐ walked away

15. ☐ raced
    ☐ chased

16. ☐ all the way
    ☐ half way

17. ☐ sad
    ☐ glad

18. ☐ stay
    ☐ leave

19. ☐ loves
    ☐ hates

20. ☐ pay
    ☐ spend

▶ **STORY QUESTIONS**

1. Why was the mailman afraid of the dog?
2. What happened when the dog growled at the mailman?
3. Why was Charlie glad to see the mailman leave?

▶ **COMPOSITION** • *Retell the story about the mailman, the bulldog, and Charlie Barnum. Look at the pictures, the key words, and the story questions for ideas.*
Begin like this: <u>Last Friday, the mailman had a terrible experience when he tried to…</u>

STORYTELLING • Personal Experiences

▶ **CLASS ACTIVITY** • *Answer the questions about the pictures.*

1. Why was the mailman scared?

2. Why was Jeff excited?

3. Why was Josie sad?

4. Why was Josie happy?

5. Why was Jane stressed out?

6. Why was Felix worried?

▶ **GROUP DISCUSSION** • *Do the pictures remind you of experiences in your life? Tell the others about a time when you were scared, excited, sad, happy, stressed out, or worried. What happened? Ask each other questions to get more information about these experiences.*

Useful expressions:

Wow!	Oh, come on.	Oh, really?	What happened then?
That's incredible!	I can't believe it.	What did you do?	I'm glad/sorry to hear that.

▶ **COMPOSITION** • *Write about an experience in your life that you will never forget.*

LIFE SKILL • Taking a Message

▶ 🎧 *Listen. Listen and practice.*

GROVER: Hello.

EDDIE: Hi, Mr. Muldoon. It's Eddie.

GROVER: Hi, Eddie.

EDDIE: Is Jamie there?

GROVER: No, she went out. Can I take a message?

EDDIE: Yes. Please tell Jamie to meet me at the Plaza Theater at 7 p.m.

GROVER: The Plaza Theater at 7 p.m.?

EDDIE: That's right.

GROVER: Okay, I'll give her the message.

EDDIE: Thanks a lot.

▶ **PHONE MESSAGES** • *Here are three messages for Jamie. Read the messages aloud.*

Jamie —
Eddie called. He wants you to meet him at the Plaza Theater at 7 p.m.
Dad

1

Jamie —
Sara called. She wants to know if she can use your computer. Her number is 726-5901.
Dad

2

Jamie —
Eddie called again. He can't meet you tonight. He has to help his mom.
Dad

3

▶ 🎧 **WRITING** • *Listen to these phone calls for Jamie. Listen again and write down the important information.*

1

2

PRONUNCIATION

▶ **A** 🎧 *Listen and repeat. Notice the pronunciation of the **-ed** endings.*

/**id**/	/**d**/	/**t**/
need**ed**	open**ed**	ask**ed**
paint**ed**	play**ed**	danc**ed**
want**ed**	show**ed**	wash**ed**
_____	_____	_____ talked _____
_____	_____	_____
_____	_____	_____
_____	_____	_____

▶ **B** 🎧 *Listen and write these verbs in the correct columns.*

talked	listened	started	finished	closed	ended
rested	introduced	called	waited	liked	smiled

▶ **C** 🎧 *What did these people do yesterday? Listen to the verb in each sentence.*

1. He _listened_ to music.

2. She _____ a chicken.

3. He _____ his mother.

4. She _____ to school.

5. He _____ the table.

6. She _____ her money.

7. He _____ for the bus.

8. She _____ the piano.

9. He _____ his teeth.

▶ **D** *Complete the sentences in Part C. Then read each sentence out loud.*

GRAMMAR SUMMARY

SIMPLE PAST TENSE Affirmative

He She I You We They	walked drove took the bus	to class last week.

Negative

He She I You We They	didn't (did not)	walk drive take the bus	to class last week.

Interrogative

Did	he she I you we they	walk drive take the bus	last week?

Short Answers

Yes,	he she I you we they	did.	No,	he she I you we they	didn't.

Questions with WHERE, WHEN, WHO, WHAT

Where did Jack go?	To the library.
When did he leave?	12 o'clock.
Who did he meet?	Jill.
What did they study?	History.

CONTENTS

Chapter

CARTOON STORY • Bruno and Marisa

▶ 🎧 *Listen and read. Then each student reads a sentence in the story out loud.*

1. Yesterday afternoon, Bruno went to the library to study.

2. He found a place to sit by the window.

3. Bruno was surprised when he saw the pretty blond girl at the same table.

4. Her name was Marisa.

5. Marisa looked up and smiled at Bruno.

6. Bruno's heart was pounding. This was his big chance.

7. Unfortunately, Marisa had to leave for her next class.

   Good-bye.

8. Bruno wanted to talk to Marisa, but he was too shy.

9. Sadly, Bruno missed his opportunity.

▶ STORY QUESTIONS

1. Was Bruno surprised when he saw Marisa at the library yesterday?
2. How did Bruno react when Marisa smiled at him?
3. Why didn't Bruno talk to Marisa when he had the opportunity?
4. How did he feel when she left?
5. What did Bruno see on the table?
6. What did he do?
7. Did Marisa wait for Bruno when he called out to her?
8. What did Marisa say when Bruno gave her the umbrella?
9. What happened then?
10. How did the story end?

▶ SHOWING INTEREST • *Marisa tells her best friend Cindy about Bruno. Cindy is very curious. What questions does she ask?*

▶ PAIR WORK • *Complete the conversation with Marisa's answers to Cindy's questions. Use your memory – and your imagination. After you finish, practice the conversation.*

MARISA: I met this amazing guy yesterday!

CINDY: Oh, really? What's his name?

MARISA: _____Bruno._____

CINDY: How did you meet him?

MARISA: _____

   _____

CINDY: What's he like?

MARISA: _____

CINDY: Are you going to see him again?

MARISA: _____

▶ 🎧 *Now listen to the conversation between Marisa and Cindy.*

CONVERSATION • Getting the Details

▶ 🎧 *Listen to the people in the pictures. Think of three questions you can ask each person to get more information. Write your questions below the pictures.*

Bruno   Peter

1. <u>What's her name?</u>
2. _____
3. _____

Jamie   Sara

1. _____
2. _____
3. _____

Max   Judy

1. _____
2. _____
3. _____

Felix   Roger

1. _____
2. _____
3. _____

▶ **PAIR WORK** • *Find a partner and exchange your lists of questions. On a separate piece of paper, write the answers to your partner's questions. Then improvise a conversation for each picture. Use some of the questions and answers you wrote down – and use your imagination!*

▶ **GROUP WORK** • *Each person tells the group about a recent event in his or her life. The others ask questions to get more information about the event.*

▶ **COMPOSITION** • *Write a short story about a recent event in your life.*

GRAMMAR REVIEW • Simple Past Tense

▶ **WRITING** • *Write affirmative and negative sentences about the people in the pictures. After you finish, read the sentences out loud.*

1. Suzi (walk) __walked__ to the market this morning. She (drive) __didn't drive__ her car because she (need) __needed__ to get some exercise.

2. The girls (make) _____ any noise when they (come) _____ into the living room. They (want) _____ to wake up their father.

3. We (go) _____ to a concert Friday, but we (enjoy) _____ it. The band (be) _____ very good.

4. David (sleep) _____ last night because he (drink) _____ a lot of coffee before he (go) _____ to bed.

5. Jenny (laugh) _____ when Marty (make) _____ a funny face in class. But the teacher (think) _____ it was very funny.

6. A lot of kids (go) _____ to a movie at the Rex Theater on Saturday. Marty (see) _____ the movie because he (have) _____ any money.

Happy Birthday!

7. Joan (give) _____ her husband a tie for his birthday. He (like) _____ the tie because it (be) _____ pink. He hates pink.

8. Mike (eat) _____ a hot dog and (drink) _____ a soda at the ball game. His girlfriend (eat) _____ anything. She (be) _____ hungry.

9. The officer (try) _____ to give the tourist directions to the post office, but she (understand) _____. She (know) _____ only a few words in English.

10. It (rain) _____ yesterday and Luisa (get) _____ wet because she (take) _____ her umbrella. She (try) _____ to stop the rain with a newspaper, but it (help) _____.

11. Lucy (go) _____ to work today because she (feel) _____ well. She (stay) _____ home and (take) _____ some medicine.

12. Mr. Valdez (complain) _____ because he (like) _____ the food they (serve) _____ at the restaurant. It (be) _____ awful.

▶ **WRITING** • *Answer the questions with adjectives such as* **wonderful, fantastic, beautiful, very bad, awful, terrible**. *After you finish, pair up and practice the conversations.*

1. Where were Ken and Suzi last Saturday?
   They were at a rock concert.
   What were the musicians like?
   They were fantastic.

2. Where was Anne yesterday?
   _____
   How was the weather?
   _____

3. Where was Mr. Posey this morning?
   _____
   How was the coffee?
   _____

4. Where were Mario and Luisa this morning?
   _____
   How was the weather?
   _____

5. Where were Mr. and Mrs. Davis yesterday?
   _____
   What were the paintings like?
   _____

6. Where was Bitsy last night?
   _____
   How was the food?
   _____

GRAMMAR • Future with *be going to*

▶ 🎧 *Listen and practice.*

Where are you going?

To the bank. I'm going to cash a check.

▶ **PAIR WORK** • *Have similar conversations.*

▶ **PAIR WORK** • *Ask and answer questions about the pictures.*

1. A: What is Mrs. Peel
      serving her guests?
   B: She's serving **them**
      some cake.

2. A: What is the salesman
      showing Maria?
   B: He's showing **her**
      some shoes.

3. A: What is Jamie
      giving Fenwick?
   B: She's giving **him**
      a bone.

4. What is Fenwick bringing
   Grover?

5. What is Ms. Standfast
   showing her guests?

6. What is Becky giving
   the teacher?

7. What is Gus serving his
   guests?

8. What is Mr. Chang
   buying his daughter?

9. What is Ana showing
   her father?

10. What is Mike bringing
    Lulu?

11. What is the clown
    giving the children?

12. What is Mrs. Anderson
    buying her son?

GRAMMAR • Quantifiers

▶ 🎧 *Listen.*   ▶ **WRITING** • *Complete the sentences with **a few** and **a little**.*

Are you ready?

Not yet. I need <u>a few</u> more minutes.

①

How's the soup?

It's good. But it needs <u>a little</u> salt.

②

Is there any furniture in the apartment?

Yes. There's a table and _____ chairs.

③

AIRPORT CHECK-IN

Do you speak English?

Yes, _____.

④

Are you going to the movies alone?

No, I'm going with _____ friends.

⑤

Do we have any food for the cat?

There's _____ milk in the refrigerator.

⑥

Grand Expectations

May I ask you _____ questions?

Okay.

⑦

Do you want sugar in your coffee?

Yes, _____.

⑧

Is there any mail for me?

Yes, _____ letters.

⑨

▶ **PAIR WORK** • *Practice the conversations.*

LIFE SKILL • Renting an Apartment

▶ 🎧 *Yesterday Daisy Miller called the manager of the Majestic Apartments about an apartment for rent. Today she's going to see the apartment. Listen. Listen and practice.*

LIFE SKILL • Renting an Apartment

①

②

③

Gordon Jackson is new in town. He's staying at the Regal Hotel. He needs to find an apartment, so he buys a newspaper and looks at the classified ads.

	CLASSIFIED ADS		
1	**GLENDALE –** $635 Single unfurn. New paint, utils. incl., pool, prkg. Xlnt. loc. Call manager 555-3528	**LAKEWOOD –** $700 Nice 1 bdrm. Lndry. A/C, balc., great view! Clean, quiet bldg. 468-2297	4
2	**GLENDALE –** $800 1 bdrm. furn., laundry, prkg. Good neighborhood, close to shopping. 555-3751	**LAKEWOOD –** $1,200 2 bdrm., 2 ba. Utils. incl., new paint, stv./frig. Near transp. Pets OK! 467-8564	5
3	**GLENDALE –** $1,150 2 bdrm, 2 ba. Utils. free, new carpet, stv./frig. Near shops & transp. 555-5097	**LAKEWOOD –** $1,800 3 bdrm. hse. Large rooms, fireplace, view, grdn. 2 car garage. 462-7329 9-5 p.m.	6

ABBREVIATIONS

A/C = air conditioning	cpt. = carpet	prkg. = parking
apt. = apartment	frig. = refrigerator	stv. = stove
ba. = bathroom	furn. = furnished	transp. = transportation
balc. = balcony	grdn. = garden	unfurn. = unfurnished
bdrm. = bedroom	hse. = house	utils. incl. = utilities included
bldg. = building	lndry. = laundry	xlnt. loc. = excellent location

PRACTICE • *Study the abbreviations and then describe the apartments in the classified ads.*

1. It's a single, unfurnished apartment. It has new paint and the utilities are included…

LIFE SKILL • Inquiring About an Apartment

▶ 🎧 *After Gordon found an apartment he liked, he called the manager. Listen. Listen and practice.*

MANAGER: Hello. Imperial Apartments. May I help you?

GORDON: Yes. I'm calling about the apartment you have for rent. Is it still available?

MANAGER: Yes, it is.

GORDON: Your ad says the apartment is seven hundred dollars a month. Does that include utilities?

MANAGER: The water is included. You pay for gas and electricity.

GORDON: Is the apartment furnished?

MANAGER: No, but there's a new stove and refrigerator.

GORDON: Good. When can I see the apartment?

MANAGER: I'm here all day. Come any time you like.

GORDON: I'll come this afternoon. My name is Gordon Jackson.

MANAGER: Gordon Jackson. Okay, see you this afternoon.

▶ **PAIR WORK** • *Have a similar conversation. Student A sees the advertisement below and calls the manager about the apartment. Student B is the manager of the apartment building.*

> **GLENDALE –** $700 1 bdrm. New carpet & paint, stv./frig. Near shops & transp. Xlnt. loc. Call manager 555-0671

STUDENT A: Ask the manager for information about the apartment. Use some of the questions below:

STUDENT B: Answer the questions about the apartment. There is no right or wrong answer.

- Is the apartment furnished?
- Is there air conditioning?
- Are the utilities included?
- Is there a laundry room?

- Is it quiet?
- Is there parking?
- What are the tenants like?
- Are pets okay?

▶ **GROUP WORK** • *What things are important to you when you look for an apartment? Make a list of the five most important things.*

HILDA AND THE CROWS

▶ **A** *Look at the picture of Hilda shaking her fist. What is Hilda's problem?*

You stupid crows! Those are my plums!

KEEP OUT!

▶ **B** 🎧 *Hilda is talking to her neighbor, Betsy. Listen.*

▶ **C** *Read these words and expressions. Is there anything you don't understand?*

crows	stupid	What's wrong?	It's terrible!	That's a great idea!
plums	precious	You look upset.	What can I do?	Where can I buy…?
plum cake	delicious	I hate it when…	I have an idea.	Sure, no problem.
scarecrow	afraid	That's not very nice.	Why don't you…?	It's a deal!

▶ **D** 🎧 *Listen again to the conversation between Hilda and Betsy.*

▶ **E** *Answer the questions about the conversation.*

1. Why is Hilda upset?
2. Does Hilda need the plums to make a dessert?
3. What is Betsy's opinion of Hilda's plum cake?
4. How can Hilda *get rid of the crows* in her back yard?*
5. Does Hilda know where she can buy a scarecrow?
6. How can Betsy help Hilda?
7. What does Betsy want *in exchange* for a scarecrow?*
8. Does Hilda accept Betsy's offer? What does Hilda say?

*get rid of the crows = make the crows leave
*exchange = to give something to someone so that they will give you something
　　　　　　　that is better for you

▶ **F** 🎧 *Listen again to the conversation.*

▶ **G** *Pair up and act out the conversation between Hilda and Betsy. Add your own ideas. After practicing for a few minutes, act out the conversation in front of the class.*

▶ **DISCUSSION** • *The crows are a pet peeve of Hilda's. Now talk about the pet peeves of the people in the pictures below. (1) Why is Jamie upset? (2) Why is the park ranger upset? Do the same things bother you?*

▶ **GROUP WORK** • *Each student tells the group about his or her pet peeve. The others give their opinions and advice. Make a list of the pet peeves in your group and tell the class.*

▶ **COMPOSITION** • *Write a paragraph about one of your pet peeves.*
Begin like this:　I hate it when…　OR　It really bothers me when…

VOCABULARY

NOUNS

air conditioning
carpet
crows
electricity
event
gas
laundry
paint

pet peeve
plums
opportunity
salt
scarecrow
tenants
utilities
vent

VERBS

cash
complain
exchange
get rid of
grab
pound
offer
shake
wake up

ADJECTIVES

amazing
available
fantastic
furnished
included
precious
recent
stupid
unfurnished

ADVERBS

happily
sadly
suddenly
unfortunately

EXPRESSIONS

I'm here all day.
Come any time you like.

I'm going to think it over.
It's a deal!

He's new in town.
This is his big chance.

I hate it when…
It really bothers me when…

PRONUNCIATION

▶ **A** 🎧 *Listen and repeat.*

/ər/

1. b<u>ir</u>d
2. w<u>or</u>d
3. l<u>ear</u>n
4. t<u>ur</u>n
5. n<u>ur</u>se
6. p<u>er</u>son
7. s<u>er</u>ve
8. und<u>er</u>
9. wat<u>er</u>

▶ **B** 🎧 *Listen and repeat.*

/ɑr/

1. c<u>ar</u>
2. p<u>ar</u>k
3. y<u>ar</u>d
4. f<u>ar</u>
5. st<u>ar</u>
6. d<u>ar</u>k
7. g<u>ar</u>den
8. p<u>ar</u>ty
9. guit<u>ar</u>

▶ **C** 🎧 *Listen to each pair of words. Listen and repeat.*

1. a. star   b. stir

2. a. barn   b. burn

3. a. heart   b. hurt

I hurt my arm.

4. a. Clark   b. clerk

Always give a firm handshake.

5. a. farm   b. firm

This donut is hard.   I heard something!

6. a. hard   b. heard

▶ **D** 🎧 Look at the words in Part C. Listen and ⟨circle⟩ the words you hear.

▶ **E** 🎧 *Listen and practice.*

1. M<u>ar</u>k's b<u>ir</u>thday p<u>ar</u>ty is on Sat<u>ur</u>day.
2. My sist<u>er</u> F<u>er</u>n is ch<u>ar</u>ming and sm<u>ar</u>t.
3. There's a l<u>ar</u>ge b<u>ir</u>d in h<u>er</u> g<u>ar</u>den.
4. B<u>ar</u>ney h<u>ur</u>t his <u>ar</u>m on the f<u>ar</u>m yest<u>er</u>day.
5. W<u>or</u>king in a b<u>ar</u>nyard is h<u>ar</u>d w<u>or</u>k.
6. F<u>ar</u>mer's h<u>ar</u>dly ev<u>er</u> w<u>or</u>k after d<u>ar</u>k.

TEST

_____ hat do you prefer?

The gray one.

_____ food do you serve?

American food.

1. a. Who's   c. Which
   b. Whose   d. What

2. a. Whose   c. How much
   b. Which   d. What kind of

3. The park is across the street
   _____ the hotel.

   a. to   c. for
   b. at   d. from

4. There are some good restaurants
   _____ this city.

   a. at   c. on
   b. in   d. to

5. "How does Felix go to work?"
   "_____"

   a. By car.   c. In the morning.
   b. On time.   d. At the bus stop.

6. "What do you do for a living?"
   "_____"

   a. I'm busy.   c. Yes, I do.
   b. I'm a banker.   d. I'm okay.

7. Mr. Summerville is a busy man.
   He doesn't have _____ free time.

   a. much   c. some
   b. many   d. no

8. We can't afford to buy new clothes
   because we have very _____ money.
   a. much   c. few
   b. many   d. little

9. _____ people take the bus
   during the rush hour.

   a. A lot of   c. A few
   b. Much   d. Some

10. There are _____ cars in the
    parking lot.

    a. a lot of   c. a few
    b. many   d. a little

TEST

Whose hat is that? It's _____.

11. a. his c. mine
    b. hers d. ours

Is this your umbrella? No, it isn't _____.

12. a. ours c. mine
    b. yours d. theirs

13. I'm going to the market
    to _____ some milk.

    a. bring c. have
    b. drink d. buy

14. It always _____ hot
    in the summer.

    a. be c. gets
    b. feel d. makes

15. English is an easy language.
    Anyone _____ learn English.

    a. can c. needs to
    b. has to d. wants to

16. My brother is lazy.
    He _____ work.

    a. can c. doesn't like to
    b. likes to d. would like to

17. Lucy is in the kitchen.
    She _____ coffee.

    a. is doing c. make
    b. is making d. makes

18. I never _____ coffee.
    Coffee isn't good for me.

    a. drink c. drinks
    b. don't drink d. am drinking

19. Hilda was happy because she
    _____ ten dollars yesterday.

    a. made c. lost
    b. stole d. found

CATS 87 | MICE 61

20. Mark was disappointed because
    his team _____ the game.

    a. didn't play c. didn't lose
    b. didn't win d. didn't score

TEST

21. "Did Donna wash the dishes?"
    "_____"

    a. Yes, she does.   c. Yes, she did.
    b. No, she doesn't.   d. No, she didn't.

22. "Did Felix buy a new car?"
    "_____"

    a. Yes, he did.   c. Yes, he does.
    b. No, he didn't.   d. No, he doesn't.

23. Milton hates to work for Ms. Krock.
    He thinks she's a bad _____.

    a. customer   c. boss
    b. employee   d. owner

24. We all make mistakes.
    Nobody's _____.

    a. happy   c. good
    b. perfect   d. wonderful

25. Mike wants to please his girlfriend.
    He's going to give _____ some candy.

    a. her   c. to her
    b. hers   d. for her

26. My brother has problems.
    I'm trying to help _____.

    a. it   c. him
    b. them   d. me

27. Linda has a lot of friends.
    She's very _____.

    a. neat   c. shy
    b. popular   d. lonely

28. We're waiting for Maynard.
    He's _____ again.

    a. early   c. late
    b. on time   d. ready

29. a. Thank you.   c. So are you.
    b. Me, too.   d. Yes, please.

30. a. Soon.   c. Okay.
    b. Later.   d. Right now.

AUDIO SCRIPT

Chapter 1 • Page 11 • DICTATION

Walk down Central Avenue two blocks to Main Street. Turn left and walk down Main Street. Lulu's Pet Shop is on the left, between Junior's Market and the police station.

Chapter 1 • Page 16 • DICTATION

I live in a pretty white house that is ninety years old. It has a big porch with flowers all around it, and there's an apple tree in the front yard. My house is on a quiet street. I like it here because my neighbors are very friendly. They always smile and say hello when they walk by my house. I know a lot of people on my street, and that makes me feel good.

Chapter 1 • Page 17 • YOUR NEIGHBORHOOD

NANCY: Hello?

JACK: Nancy, it's Jack.

NANCY: Hi, Jack. How are you doing?

JACK: Fine. I got your letter yesterday. It sounds like you live in a nice neighborhood.

NANCY: Yes, it's very nice. What about you, Jack? What's it like where you live?

JACK: It's really crowded. I live in an apartment building downtown. Everywhere you look there are people and cars.

NANCY: What are your neighbors like?

JACK: They aren't very friendly. I only know one person in my building – the manager – and he's always in a bad mood.

NANCY: Is there much to do where you live?

JACK: Let's see. There's a movie theater across the street, and there's a public library around the corner. But the best place to hang out is Central Park.

NANCY: Why?

JACK: It's the only place in the neighborhood with trees and flowers and green grass. I go there to relax.

NANCY: That sounds like a good idea. Everyone needs a place to hang out.

Chapter 2 • Page 30 • DICTATION

Mr. Little lives in a small apartment on Main Street. Every morning he gets up at 5 o'clock, puts on his old brown suit, and takes the bus to work. Mr. Little works as a secretary at the Big Balloon Company. It's a boring job. Every day he does the same thing. He types letters and answers the phone. He feels like a nobody. The other employees don't even notice him. In the afternoon, Mr. Little looks out the window and daydreams. In his dreams, he's a super hero. But his dreams don't last very long. The president of the company, Mr. Stone, doesn't like it when his employees aren't working. Mr. Stone always yells, "Get back to work!"

Chapter 2 • Page 37 • DICTATION

The room I like most in my house is the living room. I go there whenever I have some free time. I like to relax on the sofa and listen to my favorite music. I have a great collection of CDs. I also have a lot of interesting books. I keep them in a large bookcase next to the fireplace. On cold winter nights, I like to sit in front of a big fire and read a good book. At my house, the living room is the best place for me to relax and enjoy myself.

Chapter 3 • Page 50 • DICTATION

There's a good movie playing at the Plaza Theater today. It's a comedy with Lola Bankhead called *Crazy Days*. Karen wants to go and see it. But first she has to clean the kitchen and wash the dishes. Then she can go to the movies.

Chapter 3 • Page 56 • DICTATION

Mike takes good care of his health. He starts each day with a bowl of cereal, some fresh fruit and a big glass of water. Mike eats a lot of fruit and vegetables, and he drinks eight glasses of water a day. Mike also gets a lot of exercise. He goes running for an hour every morning, and he plays basketball three times a week. Mike never stays up late at night. He always goes to bed early so he can get eight hours of sleep. Mike has a lot of energy because he keeps fit.

Chapter 4 • Page 74 • MR. PERKINS

Mr. Perkins is a good employee. When he comes to work, he's always cheerful, well dressed, and on time. Every day, Mr. Perkins sits at his desk and writes business reports. He works fast, and he has a good attitude. Mr. Perkins never complains when they give him more work to do. He just smiles and says, "No problem." Everyone likes Mr. Perkins. He's the most popular person in the office.

AUDIO SCRIPT

Chapter 5 • Page 91

CONVERSATION 1

A: I plan to take my vacation next month.

B: Oh, really? **Where** do you plan to go?

A: Bora Bora.

B: Bora Bora? **Why** do you want to go there?

A: They say it's beautiful.

B: **Who** are you going with?

A: My sister. It's her idea.

CONVERSATION 2

A: I hope to buy a house next year.

B: That's great! **Where** do you want to live?

A: In the suburbs…on a nice, quiet street.

B: **What kind of** house do you want to get?

A: A traditional house with a big yard and a garden.

B: Sounds wonderful. **How much** do you want to spend?

A: Well, my limit is three hundred thousand dollars.

CONVERSATION 3

A: I'd like to change jobs. This job is boring.

B: **What** do you want to do?

A: Something interesting. I want to make a lot of money.

B: **How** are you going to find a job like that?

A: In the want ads. Maybe I can find an office job.

B: **Why** do you want to work in an office? That's not interesting.

A: It's better than this.

CONVERSATION 4

A: I don't want to live here anymore.

B: Me, neither. **Who** wants to live in a place like this?

A: It's so dangerous. I'm afraid to leave my apartment.

B: I know. But **what** can you do? **Where** can you go?

A: Well, my daughter has a large house in a nice neighborhood.

B: **Why** don't you live with your daughter?

A: I would love to.

Chapter 5 • Page 96 • CHARACTER SKETCH

MS. KROCK: Why are you so slow? You're wasting time! Time is money!

BRUNO: She's very cute, but I don't think she wants to talk with me. She doesn't even know I'm here.

Chapter 6 • Page 116 • DESCRIBING A SCENE

MELINDA: Hello. My name is Melinda Lee. I'm going to play my favorite song. It's called *Twinkle, Twinkle, Little Star*. I hope you like it.

MR. LEE: Bravo! That's my girl! Isn't she wonderful!

STUDENT: Mr. Flounder, she's making a lot of mistakes.

Chapter 6 • Page 117

DESCRIBING A SCENE

CHARLIE: Well, well. Hi, there, Mr. Mailman.

MAILMAN: Here are your bills.

CHARLIE: Don't worry about the dog. His bark's worse than his bite.

MAILMAN: Oh, no…help!

CHARLIE: There he goes again.

Chapter 7 • Page 133

CONVERSATION 1

A: What did you do yesterday, Jamie?

B: I went to the mall.

A: Did you buy anything?

B: Yes. I got a pretty orange dress.

A: When are you going to wear it?

B: This Friday. I'm going out on a date.

A: Have fun!

CONVERSATION 2

A: How was your weekend, Tony?

B: Great! I went to a party on Saturday.

A: Where was the party?

B: At a friend's house.

A: Who was there?

B: A lot of college students.

A: Did you meet anyone interesting?

B: Yeah…I met a cute blond named Karen.

A: Cool.

CONVERSATION 3

A: Did you have a good time yesterday?

B: Yeah. I went to a movie.

A: What movie did you see?

B: *King Kono*.

A: Who was in it?

B: The star was a big ape.

A: What was it about?

B: It's an adventure story. They go into the African jungle and capture this big ape.

A: Wow! Sounds exciting.

CONVERSATION 4

A: How was your weekend, Ken?

B: Terrific! I went to the beach on Sunday.

A: Which beach did you go to?

B: Laguna Beach. It was pretty crowded.

A: How was the weather?

B: Beautiful. It was warm and sunny.

A: Did you go in the water?

B: I sure did. I had a blast.

AUDIO SCRIPT

Chapter 7 • Page 134 • THE BIG GAME

The score was tied 65 to 65 and the Tigers had the ball…Our best player stole the ball from the Tigers. Suddenly, he fell and hurt his leg. The coach sent me into the game. One of my teammates passed me the ball. A player from the other team came at me. I shot the ball. The ball went through the hoop. Everyone cheered. I was a hero.

Chapter 7 • Page 135 • DICTATION

I will never forget my first day at school in America. I was very nervous because I didn't know anyone, and my English wasn't very good. The teacher, Ms. Blake, introduced me to the other students in the class. When the class ended, all of the students got up and left the room. No one came over to talk with me. I was sure they didn't like me because I was different. I walked slowly out of the room and down the hall. I felt very sad. Then, suddenly, I heard someone call my name. I turned around and saw one of the girls from my class. She gave me a big, friendly smile. I felt better right away. From that moment, I knew I wasn't going to be lonely any more.

Chapter 7 • Page 136

THE DOG AND THE MAILMAN

Last Friday, the **mailman** had a terrible **experience** when he tried to **deliver** some **bills** to Charlie Barnum. When the mailman walked **through** the front **gate**, he got a very unfriendly **greeting** from Charlie's dog. Charlie has a **mean** bulldog with **sharp** teeth and a bad **attitude**. When the dog **growled** at the mailman, the mailman got so **scared** that he **dropped** Charlie's bills and **ran away**. The bulldog **chased** the mailman **all the way** down the street. Charlie was **glad** to see the mailman **leave** because Charlie **hates** to **pay** his bills.

Chapter 7 • Page 138

LIFE SKILL • TAKING A MESSAGE

PHONE CALL 1

GROVER: Hello.

LINDA: Hello. Can I speak to Jamie, please?

GROVER: Jamie isn't here. Who's calling?

LINDA: This is Linda. Please ask Jamie to call me.

GROVER: Does she have your number?

LINDA: It's 547-8291.

GROVER: 547-8291?

LINDA: That's right.

GROVER: Okay, I'll give her the message.

LINDA: Thank you.

PHONE CALL 2

GROVER: Hello.

JACK: Hello. I'd like to speak with Jamie.

GROVER: Jamie isn't here. Do you want to leave a message?

JACK: Yes. Please tell her that Jack called. I'd like to know if she's coming to the meeting tomorrow.

GROVER: Does she have your number?

JACK: Yes, she does.

GROVER: Okay, I'll tell her you called.

JACK: Thank you.

Chapter 8 • Page 146 • MARISA AND CINDY

MARISA: I met this amazing guy yesterday!

CINDY: Oh, really? What's his name?

MARISA: Bruno.

CINDY: How did you meet him?

MARISA: At the library. I left my umbrella on the table, and he brought it to me.

CINDY: Ohh…that was nice.

MARISA: Just then, it started to rain, and we shared my umbrella.

CINDY: How romantic! What's he like?

MARISA: Oh, he's tall and good-looking, and a little shy.

CINDY: Are you going to see him again?

MARISA: Yes. We're going to meet for coffee tomorrow.

CINDY: Good luck with your new friend.

MARISA: Thanks.

Chapter 8 • Page 158 • HILDA AND THE CROWS

BETSY: What's wrong, Hilda? You look upset.

HILDA: I hate it when those stupid crows eat my plums.

BETSY: I know. That's not very nice.

HILDA: It's terrible! I need those plums to make my plum cake.

BETSY: Mmm…your plum cakes are delicious.

HILDA: But the crows are eating all of my precious plums. What can I do?

BETSY: I have an idea. Why don't you put a scarecrow in front of your plum tree? Crows are afraid of scarecrows.

HILDA: That's a great idea! But where can I buy a scarecrow?

BETSY: You don't have to buy a scarecrow. I can make one for you.

HILDA: You can?

BETSY: Sure, no problem. I'll make a scarecrow for you, and you can make a plum cake for me.

HILDA: It's a deal!

APPENDIX

Past Tense of Irregular Verbs

be	was/were	know	knew
become	became	leave	left
begin	began	lose	lost
break	broke	make	made
bring	brought	meet	met
build	built	pay	paid
buy	bought	put	put
catch	caught	read	read
choose	chose	ride	rode
come	came	run	ran
cost	cost	say	said
do	did	see	saw
drink	drank	sell	sold
drive	drove	send	sent
eat	ate	sing	sang
fall	fell	sit	sat
feed	fed	sleep	slept
feel	felt	speak	spoke
find	found	spend	spent
fly	flew	stand	stood
forget	forgot	steal	stole
get	got	swim	swam
give	gave	take	took
go	went	teach	taught
grow	grew	tell	told
have	had	think	thought
hear	heard	understand	understood
hold	held	wear	wore
hurt	hurt	win	won
keep	kept	write	wrote